From Antarctica to Zimbabwe

How I hit the reset button on my life

Dr. Quinta

Squinti Publishing
SquintiBooks.com

Copyright © 2017, Dr. Quinta

All rights reserved. No part of this book may be used or reproduced in any manner whatsoever without the written permission of the publisher and author.

This is a true story. Names have been changed to protect the privacy of individuals.

All photographs are courtesy of the author except for the photo of the *Ocean Endeavor* with a hole in its side which is courtesy of Toshi Fujimura.

Published in the United States of America by Squinti Publishing.
www.SquintiBooks.com

Library of Congress Control Number: 2017908692

(paperback)

ISBN-13: 978-1-947350-00-7

ISBN-10:1-947350-00-5

OTHER BOOKS BY DR. QUINTA
DrQuinta.com

Colombia In One Week
This book showcases the beauty of Colombia in photos taken on a one week trip. Photos were taken in Zipaquira, Bogota, Cartagena, and Medellin. These photos will make you want to visit Colombia

Antarctica In One Week
This book contains exquisite photos from Antarctica. The photos depict the wild beauty of frozen landscapes, icebergs, penguins, sea lions, and sea gulls. Buy this book to get a piece of Antarctica, the 7th continent, for yourself.

See more pictures from this trip (From Antarctica to Zimbabwe) on Instagram:
www.Instagram.com/globetrotting_engineer

To my husband, Diondré, who is my faithful cheerleader and my best friend. Thank you for always believing in me, even when I doubt myself.

"Traveling – it leaves you speechless, then turns you into a storyteller."

Ibn Battuta

CONTENTS

	The Beginning	1
1	South America	20
2	Antarctica	30
3	Europe	48
4	Africa	70
5	Asia	201
6	Oceania	226
7	North America	240
	The End	254

THE BEGINNING

The year was 2015. I was working for a company I shall call Big Oil Co, which explored for oil and gas. Things had been stressful at work for the past few months due to declining oil prices. Oil prices had dropped like a ton of bricks from over $100 a barrel to about $45 a barrel in less than a year. Nobody had seen it coming. As a result, oil companies were struggling. The higher-ups had let us know that layoffs were coming in April, but we would occasionally hear about individuals who had been laid off with no warning. Things were very tense around the office as we waited to be picked off like insignificant ants.

How did I end up here? I was born to Nigerian educators who, naturally, took education very seriously. My dad had a PhD in education, and my mother was a high school principal. Thanks to their efforts, I could read and write by age three, started school at age four, and had a small library by age five. My four siblings and I all enjoy reading to this day. One of the first books I owned was *Around the World in Eighty Days* by Jules Verne. I remember marveling at the adventures of the main character, Phileas Fogg, as he traveled around the world to win a bet. Other travel adventure books like *The Coral Island* by R. M.

Ballantyne only added fuel to the fire of my imagination.

When I was nine, my dad was transferred from Cameroon in West Africa, to Zambia in Southern Africa. It was a huge change in our lives: the food was different, the accents were different, and the weather was different. My mother and I had to figure out how to feed the family without the spices and ingredients we were used to. It was probably two years before we really settled down and started to feel at home. Ever since then, I've been unable to sit still. A wanderlust was ignited in me and I'm still always looking for an excuse to travel.

I attended college in the US, ending up with a PhD in chemical engineering. Growing up, I always wanted to be a medical doctor. After college, I decided it would be selfish for me to follow that dream as it would be seven years or more before I could help my siblings with their own schooling. So I became a PhD instead. Thanks to that decision, I was able to pay for my brother to finish high school at a private boarding school; I was able to help one sister through a BS in nursing in the US; and I was able to pay for the remaining two sisters to get through medical school in Cameroon. It is bittersweet that they get to live my dream but I'm glad we all did so well. I know it makes my parents proud and that makes me happy.

I always thought I would end up working in pharmaceuticals as that was somewhat close to medicine. While I was in grad school, I interned for Big Oil Co and I really liked the work. The people I worked with were pleasant, my supervisor was delightful, and the money was ridiculously good. I started to consider it as a serious option for full-time work. When they made me an offer, I jumped at it. The money would help a lot with my siblings' education. And that's how I ended up in the oil and gas industry.

FROM ANTARCTICA TO ZIMBABWE

My career at Big Oil Co was a roller coaster. Sometimes I really enjoyed it; other times, not so much. At this point, I was simply plodding through life. My routine was wake up, go to work, go home, rinse, repeat. I was too mentally exhausted at the end of the day to do anything useful for myself. Weekends were mainly for recuperating before work started again, too soon, on Monday. For six years, I had a successful but unfulfilling career. I felt like I was doing nothing useful with my life.

Travel was the only thing that made me truly happy. When I started my first job, everyone was talking about Ralph. Ralph had retired not two weeks before I started working there. He had done the rounds, saying goodbye to his friends and talking excitedly about how he and his wife would be driving an RV all over the US. Just two weeks later, he was dead of a heart attack. As someone just starting out in my career, this left a huge impression on me. Realizing that Ralph waited his whole life to enjoy himself, I knew I had to stop often and smell the roses.

> **You have to live life while you can because tomorrow is not promised.**

Ever since then, I made a concerted effort to take a trip outside the US at least once a year. I had some amazing trips: South Africa and Brazil for the soccer World Cup, Tanzania to climb Kilimanjaro, Peru to see Machu Picchu, Colombia to crash a wedding, etc. I was able to visit about 20 countries during my career with Big Oil Co, and that kept me going.

Around this time I went to see the dentist. I had been grinding my teeth in my sleep because of the stress. It had gotten so bad that my jaw would lock on one side and I would have trouble chewing. The dentist could tell just by looking at me which side I was having trouble with. She said the muscle was so tense that one side of my face was slightly bigger. She taught me a technique to unclench the jaw so I could eat but said the only cure was for me to stop stressing. I wondered what internal damage the stress was causing. Somehow, I had to force myself to relax. Walking away from the job would have solved the problem, but the layoff package was very generous and I was reluctant to leave all that money behind. I figured I might as well get something for my trouble.

I had lunch with one of my old managers. His entire twenty five year career had been in the oil industry, and he said his first ten years were spent in survival mode, because of constant layoffs. He advised me to come up with a step-by-step plan for how to find a new job: industries to focus on, companies and websites to apply to, colleagues to call for references, etc. He advised that if I did get laid off, I needed to go on vacation for a week or so to come to terms with it, then return and start following the job search plan. I asked him if he thought I should begin job searching before layoffs. His opinion was I should not. He gave examples of friends from his early years who found their dream jobs but were not laid off before the new job started. Some of them gave up their dream job to stay with Big Oil Co, while others had to walk away from the layoff package.

After that lunch, I was set. I didn't let anything ruffle my feathers. I made my job search plan and I finally unwound and relaxed. I took the attitude that it wasn't my dad's company so I didn't have to agree with every decision. As long as I got paid, I would do my job and do it well.

After I adopted this new attitude, I began to sleep like a baby at night. I still had people confiding in me and I still heard them out but I tried to teach them what my mentor had taught me. Some listened; most didn't. I avoided negative people like the plague, protecting the peace I had created for myself. I stopped working late, although I still did my work well. I was pleasant to everyone. I had lunch regularly with other group members, and checked on my remaining friends at the company often. Slowly but surely, the teeth-grinding stopped, and my jaw muscles unclenched.

I planned my layoff vacation, just in case. Hubby and I decided we would go to Bora Bora at the end of the year, regardless of what happened with my job. I was sitting at home looking up flights to Bora Bora when I got a WhatsApp call from my dear friend Kibibi. We had gone to primary school together and our parents had worked together back in the day. She was like a sister to me. However, we didn't see each other often because she lives in South Africa and I live in the US. So I was very excited when she told me she was in Canada. She had planned to surprise me but couldn't get a visa to the States in time.

Kibibi, or Kibs as I affectionately called her, was in Canada to take care of a friend who was undergoing cancer treatment, but she still really wanted to see me. I told her as long as her sick friend didn't mind, I would make my way to see her before she returned to South

Africa. I explained to her everything that was happening at work. I had already told her some stuff, but it's really hard to convey certain things especially when you are still coming to terms with them yourself. Since I was in a good place, it was easier to share everything with her. I also shared my new philosophy and how at peace I was with whatever happened.

I knew that layoffs for my group were scheduled for her last week in Canada. That was perfect because then I could fly to see her the day after. If by some awful miracle I didn't get my walking papers, I would simply take vacation days to see her. I bought the flight and tried to prepare mentally for parting ways with Big Oil Co.

I was laid off at 4:30 pm on a Monday in October. For the rest of the day and late into the night, I received phone calls and text messages from friends. It felt good to have people care what happened to me. I was in a daze so I appreciated now why my mentor said a preemptive step-by-step plan for job searching was necessary. When something like this happens, you are not yourself for a while, no matter how ready you think you are. I had prepared Hubby well for this day so he was not surprised. He was a little pissed though that it happened at the end of the day as that had ruined our lunch plans.

I packed for my trip to Canada. Kibs was staying with her sick friend, Sophia, and Sophia had insisted on me staying with her as well. I'm not big on staying with strangers but I decided I would test it out for Kibs' sake. If I didn't like it, I could always leave and get a hotel.

I arrived at Victoria International Airport on Vancouver

Island in the early afternoon. I spotted Kibs and she was literally hopping from one leg to another. She broke rank and ran to me. We hugged for a good five minutes. We would break apart and say how good it was to see each other, then hug again. Finally, we made our way to where Sophia was sitting. Sophia was an older lady possibly in her seventies, with short white hair. I said hello and politely thanked her for letting me stay at her house. She seemed pleasant enough and seemed to have good rapport with Kibs.

We had lunch and I ordered seafood. Kibs and Sophia were both winos, which is my term for wine aficionados, and they both enjoyed a glass of something red. My worst fears were confirmed: Canada was cold. In spite of this, I still chewed on ice cubes. Something about the texture of crushed ice on my tongue, and the cold water and ice trickling down my throat. It feels so good. After lunch, we went to Sophia's house. It turned out to be a duplex; she stayed downstairs and her sister Ruth stayed in the upstairs unit with her cat and dog.

I could smell the animals as soon as I walked in. Kibs and I were sharing Sophia's room while Sophia slept in the living room. I felt terrible but Sophia insisted it was better for her. The house was tiny and not so clean. Kibs explained that when she first arrived, the house was filthy and covered with animal poop and pee. Ruth and Sophia did not have the best relationship so even though Sophia was very weak and couldn't even feed herself, Ruth did nothing for her. Kibs cleaned the house and fed her friend and nursed her back to health. But there's something demeaning about letting someone see you at your most vulnerable. As soon as she got some strength back, Sophia scolded Kibs for cleaning her house, telling her,

"That's not why I brought you here."

Kibs left it alone after that and the house slowly got messy again. Ruth had her own medical issues which required regular treatment. Sophia would not drive her to the hospital even though Ruth had trouble with her vision after the treatments.

Me bonding with a statue outside the Empress Hotel on Vancouver Island.

I was perplexed when Kibs told me all this. Knowing how uncomfortable the situation was, why would she bring me into it? There is nothing worse than being embroiled in other people's drama. I was fighting so hard to have peace in my life; I didn't need this. Still I remained patient, knowing if things got too bad, I could leave and find a nice, quiet hotel. I stayed out of the drama but kept my eyes and ears open.

FROM ANTARCTICA TO ZIMBABWE

Vancouver Island is not the most exciting place. The top recommended activity was visiting Butchart Gardens. Unfortunately it was rainy and cold for most of my stay so we didn't go. Kibs and I stayed in most of the first day, just chatting and catching up. She runs her own travel consultancy and was working on building a website. This was year four of her business so I was concerned that she still didn't have a website. She also mentioned she was having issues with her business partner, and it was causing her a lot of anguish because they had started out as really good friends. I listened and sympathized and offered advice where I could.

Then we talked about my issues and my newly found freedom. Hubby was of the mind that I should travel for longer than a week since I had unlimited time on my hands now. As Hubby said, I had not had a break since I started college. I had gone from college to grad school to work without so much as a week off. Not that I didn't take vacations, but I never took breaks between major events like defending my thesis and starting full-time work. These kinds of breaks are really important to commune with oneself. Now that I've taken the trip and seen the benefits, I recommend everyone should take a break and clear their heads before making major changes. It took some getting used to but once I accepted that I had all the time in the world, I was only limited by my imagination.

I love to travel. At this point, I had been to every continent except Europe, Oceania and Antarctica. And still, I didn't let my imagination fly free. I thought I would go to Europe then stop in Africa for a bit then head to Asia and Australia. Because of the high cost, I ruled Antarctica as very difficult to get to, so I may as well not try this time around.

Kibs is a travel consultant, but I was hesitant to involve her in the planning of my trip. I am very picky and not so comfortable with others making choices for me. A couple years prior, I had climbed Mt. Kilimanjaro with friends. Kibs planned the trip for us and it was a logistical disaster. From rental cars lacking GPS we requested in advance, to hotels not having my reservation when I showed up, to the climbing company not being professional, there were many issues that made the trip not as enjoyable as it should have been. There were long silences on her part during the planning phase where I would have no idea what was settled and what wasn't. I tried to provide Kibs with feedback on how her poor planning had affected the trip but she didn't take the criticism well. I left it alone but I vowed to never use her services again.

As we were discussing my trip, she went into travel consultant mode and opened up her laptop, checking flights and hotels. I let her because I figured there was no harm in looking. We came up with a tentative itinerary.

Aside from travel planning, we went on a boat ride around Victoria harbor, and had a late lunch at the prestigious Empress Hotel. We mostly stayed inside after that. I tried to just enjoy my friend's company.

Finally, it was time for me to go. I left two days before Kibs was to leave so she and Sophia could have some time to themselves. South Africa was on my tentative itinerary so I knew I would likely see Kibs in a matter of weeks. This made saying goodbye easier.

I flew back home to dozens of texts and voicemails. I had kept my phone on airplane mode in Canada to prevent roaming charges.

After returning the calls, I reflected on my time with Big Oil Co. I thought about my achievements with the company and realized they were not worth much in the grand scheme of things. Outside the company, they were almost irrelevant. I certainly never met anyone and bragged about the things I had done for Big Oil Co. I started to realize that I had wasted six years by not pursuing other things besides work. It was a blessing in disguise that I now had this time to do things differently. When I first joined the company, I marveled at people who had been working there for thirty years. I couldn't imagine myself ever doing that. Yet here I was, and six years had passed in the blink of an eye. I had a second chance at life because I had the opportunity to reevaluate what I wanted to do with my life. I had no idea what I wanted to do next but I had plenty of time to figure it out.

I settled down to a routine. The agreement with Hubby was that I would not look for jobs just yet but take some time to rest and relax. I basically slept in every day, then watched TV for a few hours. Some days, I had lunch with friends. After a week, I was bored out of my mind. I decided,

"F*@# this sh*t."

I started seriously researching destinations for my trip. I decided that I would go to every continent. This meant Antarctica had to be on the list. The departure point for Antarctica was either Punta Arenas in Chile, or Ushuaia in Argentina. I did a lot of research and found that there were three ways to get to Antarctica from Argentina: fly there and fly back; fly there and cruise back or vice versa; or cruise there and cruise back. All three ways were very pricey, i.e. upwards of $8,000. Try as I might, I could not bring myself to spend that much on a single destination.

I did even more research and found that if you book a cruise close to the time of departure and in person, you could get as much as half off the price. I decided I had to try that. I would travel to Ushuaia for at least twelve days, and find a travel agency. If there were no cruises leaving within the time I would be there, I would try to fly to Antarctica instead. Failing that, I would extend my time in Ushuaia until there was a cruise leaving. My time was my own after all.

I estimated that the trip would last about three months. I had to be back in the US by early February so that Hubby and I could travel to Trinidad for Carnival. We had flights and costumes already paid for so canceling was not a good option.

I needed to book many multi city flights. I quickly found that the usual travel websites like Orbitz and even Google Flights limited the number of stops to only five. I considered using the round the world tickets offered by many airline groups but once again ran into limitations. I wanted to travel from Europe to Africa then to the Middle East but the airline systems would not allow that. There was also a limit on the number of miles I could travel. I gave up on the airlines.

Finally, I found a fantastic website, AirTreks.com, that let me plan and price up to twenty five multi-city flights. Their system allowed you to change the order of the cities to minimize the total cost of the tickets. They had travel agents available to book the flights for you. I contacted them and they set about reserving the flights. Each flight was booked separately so that missing one flight would not jeopardize the remaining ones. I was surprised to find that my flights around the world only cost around $7,000. It made me angry at myself that I hadn't done this before. I always assumed it would be too pricey.

FROM ANTARCTICA TO ZIMBABWE

Around this time, I realized that my Nigerian passport was expiring in a few days. I needed it so I could enter some countries without a visa. I had to renew it. This meant setting up an appointment with the embassy in Atlanta and hoping against hope that I got the passport back in less than a month.

The Nigerian embassy is notorious for being difficult to deal with. I looked online prior to the appointment, following all their directions to make sure I had everything I needed. And still, when I showed up, I was missing some things because they hadn't been mentioned on their website. Eventually, everything got sorted out. They did insist on giving me a new passport rather than renewing my old one. I really didn't care as long as I got it back in a timely manner. I was told it would take at least 2 weeks but could take up to a month. Expediting the application was not an option. I explained my predicament to the lady in charge and begged her to move things along quickly. She told me sternly,

> "I'll help you this time, but don't put us under pressure like this again."

I could have kissed her and she was true to her word. My passport arrived a week after I left Atlanta. I regret not taking her name. I would have loved to send her a thank you note for helping me out when she didn't have to.

The other thing holding me up was my application for Global Entry. It allows you to bypass the long lines when you go through immigration upon return to the US. It also gives TSA PreCheck access domestically so you can go through security faster, and not have to take off shoes and belts. The final remaining step was an in-person interview. That went smoothly and when the officer handed me my card, I could not stop grinning. He said dryly,

"Try to contain yourself."

I was over the moon. The trip felt real now. All I had to do was pay the travel agency and the flights would be bought, and I would be on my way.

I decided I needed a traveling companion. I'm partial to zombies and I had a zombie action figure given to me by a dear friend. However, it was too big and it needed a stand to stay upright. Something small enough to fit into my purse would be ideal. I couldn't believe I was going to be one of those people but I ended up buying a toy shih tzu and I named her Fluffy aka Fluffums aka Fluffikins. The idea was I could take pictures of sites with her in the foreground if a selfie didn't make sense. I knew I could always ask someone else to take a picture of me but other people don't always take good pictures. Finally, Fluffy was a symbol of this particular trip, proving that I had been to the places I said I was going to.

My toy shih tzu, Fluffy

FROM ANTARCTICA TO ZIMBABWE

To prepare for the trip, I checked to make sure I didn't need visas, or I could get visas on arrival with the passports I had. I checked to make sure I had any required vaccinations and I packed my yellow fever certificate showing I have been vaccinated against yellow fever. I packed light because I didn't want to check any bags. I had one small suitcase with my clothes; a waterproof backpack for my electronics; and a small waterproof sling purse for when I didn't want to bring my backpack along. I took my phone and an unlocked phone so I could buy a local Sim card if necessary. To share pictures with my friends, I created a private Instagram account just for the trip, and posted in real time when I could. I took about US$1,000 cash. I knew it wouldn't last for 3 months but I also knew I could get cash in local currencies from ATMs. I had free travel health insurance covered by AirTreks, and separate insurance through my credit card company. I took my debit card, 3 credit cards, and 3 checks, just in case. Some places I was traveling to were in the malaria zone so I brought along malaria prevention medication. I made sure to scan my yellow fever vaccination card, my passports and my Global Entry card and send copies to my phone and my email.

I booked a hotel in Ushuaia, Argentina for two nights, an Airbnb apartment in Madrid, and a hotel in London. The rest of the destinations I would take care of later.

As the departure day loomed closer, I got sadder and sadder. It was starting to hit me that I would be away from Hubby for three whole months. I also had some slight apprehension mixed with the excitement because of the unknown. My love for travel is always greater than my trepidation. In fact, the unknown is precisely what drives me to travel.

My final itinerary was US to Argentina, then Antarctica, Spain, England, Morocco, Cameroon, Rwanda, Zambia, South Africa, UAE, Thailand, Australia, French Polynesia, US, Trinidad. I built in a time buffer around South Africa. I scheduled a month in South Africa so that if my plans changed, I could move flights forward and simply spend less time in South Africa.

Locations I visited on my trip around the world

With the destinations on my itinerary, I was touching every single continent starting with South America. The order made the flights cheaper than they would have been otherwise. I had traveled to Peru, Brazil and Colombia in South America in prior years so I was content with only visiting Argentina this time around. Hubby would join me in French Polynesia and we would travel to Trinidad together. Along the way, several countries were added to my trip for different reasons. I ended up visiting 23 different countries.

Kibs called and I shared the itinerary with her. I could tell she was disappointed that I planned the trip without her. She tried to dissuade me from going to Antarctica.

"It's cold there. You will freeze,"

she said. She wasn't wrong but I wasn't going to let that stop me from going to the seventh continent.

I had goodbye lunches with friends and made goodbye phone calls. A lot of people couldn't believe I was traveling on my own. I didn't know until then that I was supposed to be afraid to travel alone, especially since I am a woman. Ironically, most of the people who said that women shouldn't travel alone were women. I've been traveling alone internationally since I was a teenager. If I waited on others, I would never go anywhere.

In the last days before the trip, I spent a lot of quality time with Hubby. He still couldn't understand why I was sad instead of happy. I just knew I would miss him a lot. The days passed quickly and before long, it was time for me to head to Argentina. In the first week of November 2015, I began my trip around the world.

Tips for international travel

- Ensure your passport is valid and has enough blank pages remaining. Extra pages can be added if the passport has not expired.

- Get visas to your destination if needed.

- Get necessary vaccinations. Some countries will not allow you entry otherwise.

- Take malaria prevention medication if going to a malaria zone.

- Take cash, debit card, and at least one credit card. You can get additional cash at ATMs in most countries.

- Get travel medical insurance.

- Carry an unlocked phone if you can, so you can use local sim cards.

- Get an International Driver's license if you intend to drive at your destination.

- Take an external charger for charging your phone and appliances when you have no access to a socket.

- Pack an adaptor for different socket types around the world. I have one that has different configurations so I can use it anywhere in the world. Therefore I only need to carry one. I recommend getting one that also has USB ports.

- Download an app that allows you to call phones in your home country for free using Wi-Fi.

- Take a GoPro camera for environments unfriendly to other cameras, like oceans and deserts.

- Buy a hybrid camera with at least one long focus lens. You will be grateful when you can effortlessly take

FROM ANTARCTICA TO ZIMBABWE

pictures in dark places, or pictures of distant objects like animals during safaris. Hybrid cameras perform like SLRs but are much lighter, making them easy to travel with.

CHAPTER 1
SOUTH AMERICA

FROM ANTARCTICA TO ZIMBABWE

The night before I flew to Argentina, I tried to check in online for my flight. It was then that I found out that I needed to pay a reciprocity fee and print out the receipt or I would not be allowed to board or enter the country. I went to the appropriate website and paid the US$160 fee, then printed out the receipt. The fee is more than one would pay for a visa to anywhere else but it is valid for ten years. I guess it's not so bad as long as you visit Argentina more than once.

The next morning, Hubby drove me to the airport. He was a little subdued. It was finally dawning on him that I would be gone for months. We held hands until I had to go through security. I hugged him tightly and cried a little, but he was very brave and hustled me along so I wouldn't miss my flight. I'm always focused and alert when I travel, especially when I travel alone. I bade Hubby farewell and focused my mind on the trip. Thus, Fluffy and I set out on our 3 month-long adventure.

I flew from Miami to Buenos Aires to Ushuaia. Ushuaia is the southernmost city in the world and is part of the region called Patagonia. It is in the province of Tierra del Fuego meaning "land of fire." The city is often called "Fin del Mundo," or "The End of the World." It is surrounded by the Martial Mountains which are part of the Andes mountain range. To the south of Ushuaia is the Beagle Channel, where Charles Darwin did some of his work on evolution.

It was late morning when I arrived. As I walked through the airport in Ushuaia, I was almost overcome with excitement. When I stepped outside the airport, I was dazzled by the sight of the beautiful, snow-covered Andes. I had done some research online and I knew it was safe to take a cab from the airport, so I did. On the drive to the hotel, my driver and I chatted haltingly about Ushuaia. My Spanish is not excellent and neither was his English, but I was able to convey how happy I was to be in

Ushuaia.

View of Ushuaia from the bay with the Andes in the background

I checked in at the downtown hotel. My room was clean and warm and very pretty. The first task was to connect to the free Wi-Fi and let Hubby know I had arrived safely. After that, I hit the pavement with my passport and credit cards, and went looking for travel agencies. In spite of how tired and hungry I was, I knew I had to find a cruise to Antarctica ASAP since I only had twelve days booked in Ushuaia. Outside, it was surprisingly warm, around 66°F, and my denim jacket felt too heavy. The receptionist at my hotel had given me a map and directed me to a travel agency which was almost ten blocks away. As I walked down the main street called San Martin, I looked about me, enjoying the sight of the mountains ever present in the background. I could also see ships unloading cargo in the bay. There were many stores on the street I was on, and the cross streets were steep because of the proximity of the mountains. Ushuaia is very walkable. During rush hour, traffic gets pretty bad downtown and walking is actually faster than driving.

I kept my eyes peeled as I walked, and I found a travel agency about five blocks from my hotel. I walked in and asked if they had any deals for cruises to Antarctica. To my surprise, they did. The *Endeavor* was operated by Quark Expeditions. It was leaving for Antarctica in two days, and tickets for the ten day cruise were roughly half price. I couldn't believe my luck.

You can't succeed if you don't try.

The ship would return on the morning of the day of my afternoon flight out of Ushuaia. The ticket would cover a bus ride to where the ship was docked, waterproof ski pants and gloves. I paid for a cabin with two beds and left with my ticket and receipt. The guy renting ski pants asked if I am an artist as apparently I was dressed like one. When I told him I'm a chemical engineer, he immediately said,

> "Antarctica is protected. Don't spill any oil while you're there."

Ouch. That hurt.

I headed back to the hotel. The temperature had dropped considerably and a cold wind had picked up. It felt like 40°F now and I felt silly to only have my denim jacket. This is how I found out that the weather can change very quickly in this part of the world. Only days earlier, there had been a big snow storm even though it was firmly spring. I realized that I was not prepared for the cold extremes.

I found a restaurant near my hotel. The waiters spoke limited English but somehow, we managed to communicate. I ordered roasted chicken with fries and a fried egg. It was on the bland side but very welcome since I was starving. I returned to the hotel, took a shower and went to sleep.

The following morning, I had the free continental breakfast at the hotel, then chatted with the receptionist about activities in the area. I booked a boat tour of the Beagle Channel. Before the tour started, I had my passports stamped with a free "Ushuaia, Fin del Mundo" stamp.

Faro Les Eclaireurs Lighthouse in the Beagle Channel

The tour was interesting. The boat was warm and comfortable, with bathrooms and snacks on board. The view of Ushuaia from the Channel was breathtaking with the mountains in the background. We saw the Faro Les Eclaireurs Lighthouse, and many sea lions and cormorants. We stopped at Karelo Island and walked around for about 20 minutes admiring the unique flora.

I should mention that the wind was biting. I decided that upon my return to the city, I would buy a warmer jacket. I knew from my research that the cruise would provide winter jackets for Antarctica so I had been counting on using that, and had minimized the number of warm clothes I brought. I also realized around this time that my boots were also too heavy. I would need a lighter, more comfortable pair. I decided to stop at the sports shops on my way back to the hotel.

I met a lovely pair of older ladies on the boat. We started chatting and I shared my story with them. They shared similar stories with me. A resounding piece of advice they gave me was to list what I enjoyed doing and then find a job that allowed me to use those skills. As one of them said,

> "I would have never imagined I would be working in my current industry but I love it."

Words to live by. I was desperate to find something I would love in this life, and it was wonderful to learn that others had been successful.

Sea lions in the Beagle Channel

After the tour finished, I hit the streets and bought a fleece, a winter jacket, gloves, a hat, thermal underwear, and booties. Bear in mind, prices have the dollar sign even though they are in Argentine pesos. The first time I looked at a price tag, I almost passed out. A thousand dollars for a pair of thermal bottoms? After converting to dollars, it was more realistic although still expensive. I was exhausted by the end of my shopping spree since I walked everywhere in those heavy boots of mine. Stores were starting to close, and the sun was going down. I picked up some food to go. Just outside my hotel, a woman broke away from her husband and daughter and came up to me. She grabbed my face and exclaimed,

"Ay! Que linda! How pretty!"

Then she kissed my cheek soundly. That's when I knew it was time to call it a day. I politely said,

"Gracias."

Inwardly, I was thinking many impolite things but I could see she meant no harm. I pulled my face back from her grasp, and entered my hotel. I understood she was paying me a compliment but I'd had a long day and just didn't know how to respond to someone grabbing my face. It has remained etched in my memory as one of the strangest things to happen to me.

My overall impression of Argentinians is that they are friendly and helpful. In spite of the language barrier, I was able to get help when I needed it. The workers at the hotel and the tours spoke excellent English. When I had issues, I would use language apps on my phone to try to bridge the gap. Argentina appears to be very European compared to the other parts of South America I have been to. Some Spanish words are even different there. For example, rather than *baño* for restrooms, they use *sanitario*, which seems really formal.

The cruise left for Antarctica the following afternoon but before that, I took a tour of Tierra del Fuego National Park, which is roughly 7 miles outside Ushuaia, and rode the Fin del Mundo train. At the time, they were only accepting

MasterCard and American Express for the train ride. Lucky for me, one of my cards was a MasterCard. The ride went through the forest and stopped at Macarena Falls. The train ride and the forest reminded me very much of the train ride through the Sacred Valley in Peru to Machu Picchu, complete with the horses and rivers along the way.

After the train ride, a bus took us through the Tierra del Fuego National Park, stopping at Lake Verde and Lapataia Bay. The entire tour lasted about 5 hours and was very enjoyable. I got to test out my warm gear and found it worked very well. Although it was cold out, I remained comfortable.

The Fin Del Mundo train

After the tour, I was dropped off at my hotel. I checked out and took a cab to where the bus to the ship would leave from. I was so nervous about missing the ship that I got to the bus stop an hour early. My travel agent showed up to make sure all her clients were waiting at the right place and got on the right bus. There was myself, a couple from Australia, another Australian guy, and a young man from China. The Chinese guy had finished college and had been traveling for a year. I was stunned. I had thought three months was a long time. I asked how he was financing his trips and he said his parents were paying for it. Lucky him. The single Australian traveled on his own ship with a crew around the world. Once again, I felt like my imagination had let me down. These people were doing things that I had never even dreamt of. Clearly, I needed to push myself to dream bigger.

After the travel agent left, we did get on the wrong bus as apparently there were two ships leaving that day. Fortunately, the conductor asked to make sure we were all going to the right place. As we were not, we got off the bus and pulled our luggage off, hanging our heads in shame. No matter, our bus showed up shortly after. This time, we knew to ask what ship it was bound for before we got on.

The bus pulled up to the *Ocean Endeavor* and I thought my heart would burst out of my chest. Imagine that something you had dreamed about for a long time was finally within your grasp. I couldn't stop smiling.

Tips for travel to Argentina

- Pay the reciprocity fee and print out the receipt or you will not be able to enter Argentina. The physical receipt will be handed over to immigration authorities.

- If traveling to Ushuaia in the spring or winter, dress

warmly. In the spring, be prepared for sudden weather changes.

- The charm of Patagonia lies in the outdoors. Wear reasonable hiking shoes.

- Brush up on your Spanish.

CHAPTER 2
ANTARCTICA

FROM ANTARCTICA TO ZIMBABWE

My first impression of the crew was that they were friendly and very professional. In the days to come, I would also add competent to the list, which was reassuring since we were traveling through one of the most inhospitable regions in the world. Come to think of it, I've never understood why there are indigenous people on every continent except Antarctica. For instance, Eskimos live in the Arctic, which seems to me similarly hostile. Humans have been able to survive everywhere, no matter how hot or cold, vast or isolated. Yet, Antarctica remains mostly uninhabited.

As on every cruise, we had a safety meeting soon after we boarded. The expedition team introduced themselves and explained the emergency evacuation procedures to us. The team had really good rapport amongst themselves and seemed to really enjoy what they were doing. I was happy to see that most of them had related professional degrees such as geology.

This trip was the maiden voyage of the *Ocean Endeavor* to Antarctica. The ship had roughly 9 floors, a sauna, a gym, and a pool. There were a couple of lounges, one of which always had hot beverages. One of the lounges had a disco ball and became the venue for several parties we had on board.

I was surprised to find that there were many young people on board. To my added surprise, many were also women traveling alone. For them, as for me, this trip to Antarctica was a dream come true. There were about 165 passengers in total but the ship could hold up to 199 passengers. I was lucky enough to be assigned a cabin on my own. It was on the outside so it had a porthole. It was possible to cover the porthole to prevent light from coming in but I always kept it open. That's how I found out the sun rose really early, around 3 am. I would always wake up with a start in the middle of the night, but I couldn't bring myself to cover up the porthole.

The *Ocean Endeavor* anchored off the Antarctic Peninsula

It was warm and very dry on the ship. I did laundry occasionally and the clothes were always dry within a few hours. For health reasons, everyone always received a squirt of hand sanitizer before entering the dining room. This led to me having very dry and chapped hands but no one fell sick so it was worth it. My lips would get so chapped that I resorted to always wearing lipstick, because it does a good job of keeping the lips moisturized.

The food was very good and the service was excellent. Breakfast and lunch were buffet style, while dinner was on a menu. One night, again as on most cruises, the Captain came down from the control room and had dinner with us.

I got to try both vegemite and marmite which are breakfast spreads made from yeast extract. They are favorites in

Australia and New Zealand respectively. There's a great rivalry about both but in my opinion, they're both an acquired taste.

The cruise provided us with warm jackets and liners for the landings. They were a bright yellow to make us easier to see against the snow. Rain boots were also supplied to everyone. We would disinfect our boots before leaving the ship to prevent contamination of Antarctica, and after returning to the ship. All our equipment and clothes were checked to ensure they did not have anything like seeds that could be contaminants.

Before the landings started, we would have lectures on the flora and fauna, and geology of Antarctica. When we had landings, we would wake up early to have breakfast, cruise around the island in boats called Zodiacs for an hour, then spend about an hour and a half on land before heading back to the ship. The passengers were split into three groups: Gentoo, Adelie, and Chinstrap, which are different types of penguins. Two groups would cruise while one group landed since Antarctica is protected and there is a limit on the number of people allowed on land at one time.

Early November is the start of summer on Antarctica. Our ship was among the first 2 cruise ships to travel to the seventh continent that season. It is impossible to travel to Antarctica before November as there is too much ice. In early November, the ice and snow were still on the ground and the penguins were just starting to build their stone nests. Later in the season, tourists can see the eggs, and later still, the penguin chicks. However, later in the season the snow has melted and the ground is muddy. It makes for less spectacular pictures.

Other wildlife we saw included seals, cormorants, gulls, terns, sheath bills, whales and dolphins. Sheath bills are land birds that scavenge and eat penguin guano.

From left to right: Adeli, Chinstrap and Gentoo penguins

Extra activities were offered for a fee, including kayaking, paddle boarding, and camping overnight on Antarctica. The kayaking was sold out by the time the cruise started. A lottery system was used to fill the other activities. I did not win the paddle-boarding lottery, and I decided not to participate in the camping since I am allergic to the cold.

The route to Antarctica required us to go through the

famous Drake Passage, which connects the Atlantic and Pacific Oceans. It is well-known for high waves and strong winds. Thus, we were advised to take sea sickness medication early, if we had it. The ship's doctor had some on hand for those who hadn't brought any on board. I've never been prone to motion sickness, so I decided to try my luck and not take any medication.

It took two days to cross the Drake. I was constantly woken up by my mattress sliding across the bed. Anything that wasn't tied down fell to the floor then slid around. During dinner on the second night, the waves got so rough that waiters and dishes fell to the floor. Fortunately for us passengers, the tables and chairs were chained to the ground. We tipped over but didn't fall, but we still got food and drinks spilled all over us. Walking around the ship was tricky and required holding on to walls and railings. Many were seasick and confined to their cabins. I was lucky and only experienced slight queasiness especially at night when my bed was being rocked about. It really made me respect the explorers who went before us: Ernest Shackleton, Walter Scott, and Robert Falcon. Surviving the Drake Passage is a rite of passage when cruising to Antarctica.

The calm after we passed completely through the Drake Passage was almost surreal. Our route was Drake Passage, Aitcho Island, Half Moon Island, Deception Island, Cuverville Island, Paradise Harbor, Neko Harbor, Errera Channel, Danco Island, Wilhelmina Bay, and finally, back through the Drake Passage to Ushuaia.

Cuverville Island was my favorite. The weather was perfect. It was bright and sunny, and therefore warm, around 50°F. My group, Gentoo, cruised around the island before disembarking. The cruise was very interesting.

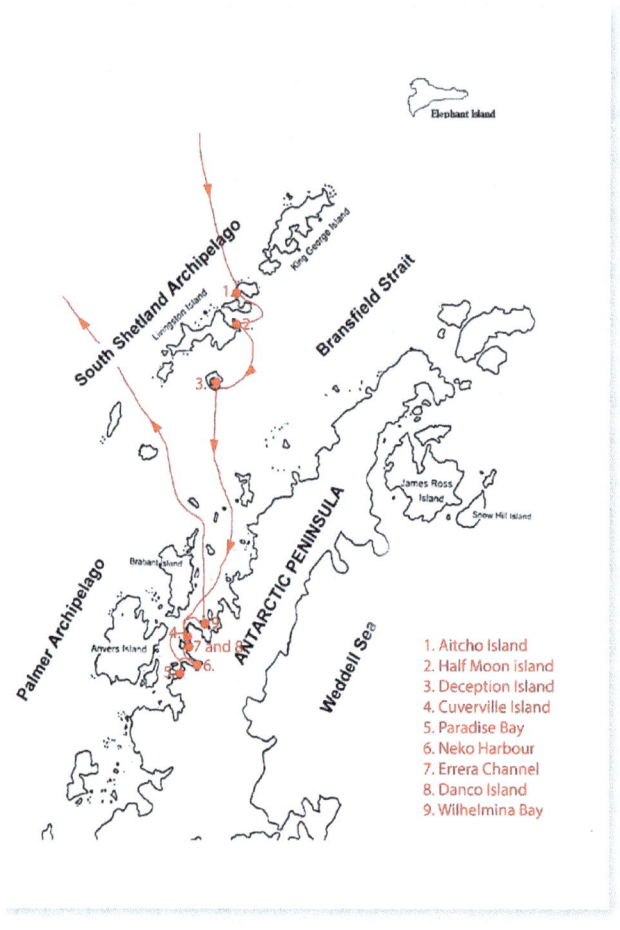

The route taken by the *Ocean Endeavor*

Rafts of gentoo were porpoising to the island in neat lines, one after the other, or all next to each other. They would often curiously follow our Zodiac, or small boat, and then abruptly change direction when we stopped. We saw dozens of gentoo penguins porpoise onto the island, and clamber onto the ice. We saw a single adelie penguin among the gentoo on the island. I wondered how he had ended up there and where the rest of his colony was.

The brightness of the sun made all the colors around us more intense. The blues in the icebergs were incredible. Because the bay around the island was shallow, we were often able to see the pebbles at the bottom. The reflection of sunlight off the snow caused a lot of red eyes among us. I wore contacts and sunglasses, and that helped a great deal. Unfortunately, my camera compensated for the brightness, and I often had to take the sunglasses off to see the image on the camera screen clearly.

Seal napping on the ice in Antarctica

When we disembarked onto the island, I simply sat down in awe and watched the penguins for a while. I found myself falling in love with them. I never cared much for them before but they are now my favorite creature. The migrating rafts of penguins were really interesting to watch, and so I did that for a while. Eventually I sat down near the path the gentoo had to take to get to the rest of the colony from the sea, and took pictures as they walked by me. The rules were we had to stay 5 meters from them but it was alright if they came to us. I watched them court each other, scuttle past me, dive into the water, clamber up from the water, freeze in place. The penguins would poop as they walked and the snow around their colonies was stained red, like the krill that they eat. I could have stayed there all day watching them. The sun being out made a tremendous difference. My fingers did not get cold at all and taking pictures was a pleasure.

After lunch, we boarded the Zodiacs and went cruising in Paradise Bay around the island, and this time, the weather was completely different. It was cold, and the wind was strong and biting. We saw the Brown Station which is a research station belonging to Argentina. Apparently, in 1984, the doctor on the base received word that his wife wanted a divorce. He spent a year at the station as his contract demanded. When the supply ship came, there was not a replacement doctor on board, though there should have been. This meant he would have to stay another year on the base. The poor doctor was desperate to save his marriage. He set the base on fire so they would all have to be removed. Unfortunately for him, his punishment was another year on the base. Needless to say, his marriage did not survive.

The weather in Antarctica can change at the drop of a hat. I was so miserable on the Zodiac that I took far fewer pictures. My fingers were so cold, I really didn't want to take them out of my pockets. We saw lots of interesting glaciers, icebergs, and lichens. We also saw cormorants and Antarctic terns. Some of the Zodiacs were fortunate enough to see a school of about seven beaked whales but they were gone by the time we got to the spot. By the time we made it back to the ship, I was miserable with cold. After we disinfected our boots, scrubbed them and took them off, my friends and I went to the sauna and warmed ourselves up. The wind grew stronger that evening, and it started to snow. Camping was postponed to the next night.

Antarctic kelp gulls

We sailed into Neko Harbor on November 13, 2015. While the weather wasn't as great as on Cuverville Island, it was good enough to allow us to enjoy the several colonies of penguins on the island. I got so wrapped up in the gentoo that I missed my cruise around the harbor. I saw them courting, mating, building nests from stones, stealing stones from each other, and chasing each other. I climbed to the top of the island and was lucky enough to see an iceberg break off from a glacier.

Several people got snow blindness. Mostly, they did not have sunglasses with them. The snow was so bright that my transition glasses were completely black. A young lady from Calgary had to skip most of the day's activities including meals because she got snow blindness and her eyes were in a lot of pain.

That night, I had dinner with Alex, a doctor from The Netherlands and learned quite a lot about himself and his family. He is a urologist, specializing in prostate oncology.

He had the most hilarious stories about objects he has pulled from inside his patients. We sat next to a group of Chinese tourists and I was astounded to see that they had brought their own food on board, and it was cooked for them at every meal. The explanation was that they found western food so strange to the taste that they couldn't eat it.

Camping was canceled that night because it was getting windy and snowy. The campers had the option of camping on deck in their special sleeping bags.

That night, we made merry. After one of the Expedition team played guitar and sang original songs, he set up some music in the Nautilus Lounge. Danny, an older gentleman from Houston, started dancing on the dance floor and slowly pulled us all on with him. Everyone had a great time. Ali, a girl from China, showed up wearing a penguin costume. Another guy, Brad from Colorado, had a lot to drink and turned out to be a jolly drunk. He danced more than the rest of us combined.

I stayed until 1 am then retired to my room. The dancing had been so intense that I had sweated through all of my clothes. So, I spent the next 30 minutes washing my clothes and taking a shower.

At breakfast the next morning, I sat down with Ali, the penguin girl. She had been traveling for 10 months through South America at that point. I was so fascinated with her. Before this cruise, I had thought three months was a long time to travel but I was meeting so many people who had been on the road for months and even years. Ali was taking a gap year after finishing school. She was a translator and was paying for her travels by translating for others. She helped translate instructions and lectures for the Chinese passengers on behalf of the crew.

After Danco Island, we cruised around Wilhelmina Bay. The weather was terrible that afternoon. Cold, felt like 20°F, windy and it was starting to snow. The ride around the bay was miserable as a result. I couldn't wait to get back to the ship. We cruised around the wreck of the Governøren, a whaling factory ship. It was full of whale oil which caught fire during a party and sank in 1915. The captain and the crew all survived and were rescued by a nearby whaling ship.

Zodiacs around the wreck of the Governøren

We returned to the ship with numb faces and fingers. The polar plunge was scheduled for later that day. This consisted of jumping into the Southern Ocean with a harness attached to one's waist. Considering how bad the weather was, and the snowflakes were getting thicker by the minute, I assumed the plunge would be canceled. However, we had had so many activities canceled that the Expedition team decided to go ahead with the plunge. Alex and I had an agreement that if I did the plunge, he would too. He actually said out loud that he didn't think I would do it since I hate the cold so much. Little did he know that I love adventure even more than I hate cold. And because I jumped, he had to also.

The anticipation was intense. We lined up in the locker room and were let through in small groups. When Alex and I finally got to the front, my heart was pounding out of my chest. There was the question now in the fore of my mind,

> "Why am I doing this?"

That question never needs a good answer. I was doing it because I wanted to experience something most people in the world will never get to do. That was reason enough for me.

I took off my bathrobe and flinched as the biting cold air hit me. The harness was fastened around my waist and I moved closer to the steps. The cold wind, the cold water beneath my feet, the choppy waves, the thick snow, and the floating icebergs made me feel like I was in a dream. When I got to the edge, the Expedition team members told me to jump to the right so that the left flowing current would bring me back to the ship. I took a deep breath and jumped. The water was around 33°F. The iciness of the water spurred me to find the steps as quickly as possible. The team helped haul me out of the water. As soon as I got out, I felt like a thousand ice cold needles were sticking me in my back. I was chilled to the core. My friends and I ran to the locker room, downed shots of bourbon, then booked it to the sauna. Other people ended up in the pool which was heated for this one day only. I felt like a champion and I was so proud of all of us. It seems simple in retrospect: just jump, but the courage it takes to do things like this can be transferred to other areas of one's life.

> **Overcoming our fears and having the courage to plunge into the unknown is**

how we can live life more fully.

That night, we headed north back to the Drake Passage and celebrated the trip by throwing a party and dancing all night. Dancing was tricky since the sea was tumultuous as we sailed through the Drake Passage. Around 3 am, I and a few others were dancing in the Meridien Lounge on the ninth floor. We felt the ship lurch as if we hit something and then saw a big iceberg float past. The wind was going strong and the snow was falling thick and fast. One of the Expedition team members went outside to investigate but visibility was too low. We waited for an announcement but none came so we assumed everything was okay. We continued the party. Now I understand why people on the *Titanic* didn't panic as soon as they hit the iceberg. You just assume that those in charge know what they're doing and they will tell you if there is trouble. Around 4 am, as I headed to my cabin, I did notice that the ship had stopped rolling even though we were still going through the Drake Passage. I slept well, with the bliss of ignorance.

Around 10 am, we were called to a meeting and informed that the ship had slowed down and changed course due to damage sustained that night. It turns out that the iceberg created a long gash in the outer hull just above the water line. Luckily there was no damage to any passenger cabins. We were informed that it would take until midnight to patch up. We changed course to westward to shelter the damaged side until it could be fixed. There was the possibility of the ship not returning to Ushuaia on time. However, the team informed us that alternate arrangements would be made if we missed any connecting flights, etc.

The hole torn by an iceberg in the hull of the *Ocean Endeavor*. Photo courtesy of Toshi Fujimura

I was supposed to fly out of Ushuaia on the same day we returned. If we were late, I would miss my flight to Buenos Aires, then Madrid. My Airbnb in Madrid was already booked and paid for so I would lose on that as well. I kept all this in mind but didn't panic. If the company was willing to compensate me for the inconvenience, or make alternate arrangements for me, then I was okay with that. It was interesting to see the reactions of the people around me. Anna, a nurse from Austin, was so convinced that we wouldn't make it that I started to question myself and my calm. Maybe I should be more concerned. I thought about it and realized there was literally nothing I could do about it, so there was no point in stressing. Until then, the professionalism of the crew and expedition team had made me trust them and I saw no reason to stop now.

I did realize that Hubby didn't know the name of the ship or the company I had booked with. I resolved to do better next time and ensure he knew where I would be at all times, just in case anything happened. Internet was available on board for a price but all bandwidth was reserved for the captain and crew to communicate with land until the repairs were completed.

The work was finished that day ahead of schedule and we headed east then north through the Drake Passage.

I had such a blast on the trip that I visited the gift shop and spent a small fortune on souvenirs. I bought penguin ice cube trays, t-shirts, sweatshirts, and postcards. I sent one postcard to myself and one to Hubby. My card read,

> "You're one of the bravest souls I know. I'm proud of you for pushing yourself to accomplish more than most people even dream about. Keep pushing because there's always more to see and do. But take this moment to stop and smell the roses. The sky may be the limit for some. But not for you."

The card to Hubby thanked him for encouraging me to go on the trip. I sent the third and final one to a former work colleague, because he asked nicely. The crew would mail the postcards from the post office on Antarctica. It took almost five months for them to arrive and I made it back to the US before they did.

At the last breakfast, I chatted with one of the Expedition

Team members. Her story was an inspiring one. She had sailed to Antarctica as a passenger the year before. She enjoyed herself so much that she went back to Denver, quit her job, then returned as a team member. I was so impressed, inspired, and encouraged by her story. It really helped me see that anything could be possible if I just tried.

We made it back to Ushuaia on time despite the repairs. Leaving a cruise ship is always hard. First you're waking up really early in the morning, usually after a late night as you try to enjoy the last night of the cruise. Second, you have to say goodbye to people you've grown close to. Finally, you are leaving excellent food and service behind. No more being waited on hand and foot. So, it was with a heavy heart that I disembarked. It didn't help that we had to have our bags scanned at the harbor before we could leave. The drug-sniffing dogs really brought us back to reality.

It was cold and rainy in Ushuaia. We arrived around 8 am and my flight left around 3 pm. I stashed my luggage at a location provided by the cruise company. Since I now had more items than could fit in my luggage, I took the extra things including the jacket from the cruise, put them in an extra bag and mailed it to myself in the US. I returned the waterproof gloves and pants and then checked in with my travel agent to tell her how the trip went. Afterwards, I ran into Dave, the older Australian gentleman from the cruise who sails around the world, and we had lunch together. Then I picked up my luggage and took a cab to the airport.

Tips for travel to Antarctica

- Get in shape. There is a lot of clambering through snow and up hills. It's not mandatory to be in shape but it helps tremendously.

- Take sunglasses and use them. Snow blindness is no joke.

- Pack top and bottom thermal underwear, thick socks and liner gloves. Waterproof gloves and pants and usually provided by the travel agency.

- Pack a warm winter hat that also covers your ears.

- If you are prone to motion sickness, take sea sickness medication with you.

- Take plenty of moisturizing lotion and lip balm.

- Pack sunscreen and use it.

- Make sure you have enough space to pack the bulky winter jacket provided by the cruise ship.

CHAPTER 3
EUROPE

My next destination was Madrid, Spain, via Buenos Aires. My seatmate was from the Philippines and he did show lightings on cruise ships. He'd just disembarked from Ushuaia and was on his way to Miami to join another cruise. He worked six or seven months out of the year. Once again, I was impressed by the possibilities in life if only one is flexible. The cruise life began to look exciting but it didn't seem quite right for me.

Somehow I missed the fact that there was a technical stop in Trelew before Buenos Aires. I slept until the plane arrived in Trelew then got off the plane groggily. As I walked outside the airport, I realized nothing looked familiar. On my way to Ushuaia, I had flown through Buenos Aires. I had had to leave the international terminal, walk outside for almost twenty minutes to get to the domestic terminal. Now, as I looked around, I realized this did not look like Buenos Aires. I went back inside and inquired, and fortunately, I was put back on the plane before the new passengers boarded. I felt like an idiot, but trust me, I did not make that mistake again.

I had four hours to kill at the airport once I arrived in Buenos Aires. As I was roaming the airport, I ran into a contingent of passengers from the cruise returning to the US. We had a good time chatting and catching up. Time came for my flight and I accidentally left my suitcase behind when I went to line up to board. It might have been because I was so tired. I had a nagging feeling that something was off. I was used to having my backpack and my suitcase but I suddenly felt too free. I finally realized my mistake and went back in shame to grab my suitcase. I share these stories because I know these things happen to others. You are not alone.

Compared to the flight from Ushuaia to Buenos Aires, Buenos Aires to Madrid was uneventful. I sat next to an older gentleman. His friends were all around us, and like most other Argentinians I had come across, were very courteous. They helped me put my bags up and made sure I woke up at meal times. They were really very sweet and I wished my Spanish was better so I could get to know them better. I was exhausted from too many late nights on the ship so I slept most of the flight. The flight was over twelve hours long so I got plenty of sleep, uncomfortable though it was.

Spain

The Museo del Prado in Madrid

After I arrived in Madrid and went through immigration, I took a cab to my Airbnb apartment in central Madrid. I chose Airbnb over a hotel because many hotel reviews warned of things being stolen from hotel rooms. I didn't want to deal with losing anything especially at the beginning of such a long trip. I carefully read over reviews for various Airbnb apartments in Madrid before I made my final decision. My hostess had many excellent reviews. I booked the entire apartment because I like my privacy.

My hostess gave me the rundown on the neighborhood but I didn't hear anything that sounded exciting. It mostly involved going to museums and I am more of an experience or adventure person. After she left, I took a long, hot shower. My hostess had left fruit, tea and pastries so I was able to eat and drink before I crashed for the night. The next morning, I woke up starving. I walked around my neighborhood, exploring. I found a bar/restaurant and ordered some food. Just like in Argentina, the food was somewhat bland but I gobbled it up.

After Argentina, I was originally supposed to fly to London with a brief stopover in Madrid. My travel agent suggested spending a few days in Madrid and I agreed. Madrid was a huge let down after Antarctica. To be fair, I was there for two nights only. How can museums and old buildings compare with natural beautiful landscapes, icebergs and cheeky penguins? It's possible that Madrid is a lovely city but I was quite bored. I would recommend that after Antarctica, wait a few months before visiting anywhere else. Your idea of beauty will be skewed for a while.

On the bright side, it was much warmer in Madrid, approximately 68°F, compared to Ushuaia and Antarctica. The sun was out and walking around was very pleasant. The highlight of my trip to Madrid was Fluffy and I sitting on a bench at the Plaza de Murillo, basking in the sun. I was so happy to be warm again.

There were several policemen and police dogs around the Plaza. I felt better when I saw two old ladies chatting with the police and petting one of the dogs. This was a few days after terrorist attacks in Paris, and Europe was on high alert. I started to rethink my plans to visit Paris.

My Airbnb apartment was close to the Museo Nacional del Prado which houses a huge collection of Spanish art. I was lucky enough to visit on a day when admission was free, since it was the anniversary of the museum. I spent a few hours looking at the mostly religious paintings.

After a couple of hours, I left and walked until I found a café. The hot chocolate I ordered was as thick as batter, and very sweet. It was like a lot of melted chocolate. There must have been some kind of misunderstanding, surely. I must have ordered the wrong thing. I called it a day and returned to my apartment.

I have no regrets about visiting Madrid. At least now I know it's not my kind of place. I've been told other places in Spain are much more exciting. I plan to visit those places next time I'm in Spain.

At the airport, security was very tight. The first time I went through the scanners, I took my laptop out of my backpack. I was sent back because there was something on the screen that looked unusual. I removed my GoPro camera, hybrid camera, kindle, and iPad, and then went through again. Yet again I was sent back and I finally realized that the numerous charging cables for my appliances were the problem. They probably looked like a suspicious device with many wires attached to it. I took them all out and finally made it through security. I said goodbye to Madrid and headed to London.

England

The Great Bath, a Roman bath house in Bath, England

I arrived at Gatwick Airport in London around 9:30 in the morning. The passport control agent was very friendly, which in my experience is unusual. We chatted about my trip around the world and he wished me all the best.

I had the option of taking either the train or a cab into London since Gatwick is on the outskirts. I ended up taking a cab for the hour-long drive to my hotel near Victoria Station.

The cabbie was as friendly as the immigration agent. I hadn't known what to expect but I was happy that Londoners were so pleasant. It certainly helped that we spoke the same language. Again, we discussed my trips and my concerns about being jaded after Antarctica. He gave me great advice. He said,

"Try to find something special about

each place."

I couldn't help but agree with him. Some places would be amazing, others less so, but each place had to have something unique. I stored his advice at the front of my mind and drew on it whenever I was discouraged or taking things for granted.

I checked into my hotel for a week. I loved my hotel. Space in London is a premium and the hotel room reflected that. It was compact and well designed to maximize effective use of the available space. I thought my room was just enough space for one, but it was the largest room size the hotel had. I could only imagine what the regular rooms looked like. The bed was pushed all the way to the wall. Next to it was a small desk with drawers. There was a coffee pot and cup in one of the drawers. The bathroom was handicap accessible so it was reasonably spacious.

My original plan was to fly from London to Poland and Germany to see friends, then return to London and fly from there to Morocco. However, the cold in London gave pause to my plans. I figured it would be just as cold in Germany and Poland. Fortunately, I hadn't bought the flights yet so I canceled my plans. You're probably wondering why London cold would be bothersome after a trip to Antarctica. The cold in Antarctica was dry. The cold in London is a damp cold that seeps through your clothes and wraps around you lovingly, chilling you to the bone. The boisterous winds didn't help. I was miserable. Even indoors, it was cold. I often had to keep my jacket on in restaurants to keep from shivering.

I often had lunch at a Chinese restaurant near my hotel. One of the waitresses was also an avid traveler. Her last trip had been a year in India. She returned to London when her funds were running low. Her plan was to work for a year then return to Asia. I was blown away by her dedication to travel. Hopefully, I could gain the courage to live like that someday.

A buddy of mine, Teddy, was coincidentally in London for a day, on his way to Madrid from the US. We met up and had dinner at a pub, as one should when in London. We had fish and chips, of course, and some excellent cider. Again, I was impressed by how friendly the waitress was.

I did quite a bit of walking around the area near my hotel. I got thoroughly lost, so I got to know the area really well. I found a tour company and booked a tour of Windsor Castle, Stonehenge and Bath for the following day.

The day of the tour was bitterly cold. Unfortunately for me, the tour required a lot of outdoor walking. The first stop was Windsor Castle where we had a couple of hours to wander around. The castle tour was very much like visiting a museum. I'm glad I went but I wouldn't go again.

Stonehenge was next and that was more interesting. It is dated as being 5,000 years old because that is the age of bones found at the site. I find that troublesome because finding 5,000 year old bones in the foundation of my house doesn't prove that my house is 5,000 years old. No one knows the purpose of the stones and many theories have been put forward, chief among which is that Stonehenge was a burial site. In any case, it was cool to see the stones that I'd read so much about. They were roped off preventing people from touching them or chipping pieces off, which used to happen. I've read that some people feel a spiritual connection to the stones. I closed my eyes and tried to feel the power that is supposed to emanate from the stones, but I felt nothing. Maybe the ropes kept us too far away.

Fluffy at Stonehenge

The final stop on the tour was the city of Bath where we stopped at the Roman baths. They were founded around naturally occurring hot springs which were thought to have healing powers. The baths were well-preserved although a little stinky. We toured the museum at the bath. One funny thing I learned was that if someone lost something, they would write down the name of the suspected thief, and offer it to the gods, asking them to curse the thief. Judging by the number of names, there were a lot of thieves in that little town.

The Roman temple in Bath was dedicated to Sulis Minerva, the goddess of healing. A bronze sculpture of the head of the goddess is on display at the museum. I was struck by this impressive sculpture which suggested an equally impressive goddess.

Afterwards, we were bussed back to London. My biggest complaint about the tour is that we didn't have enough time to explore Windsor Castle and Bath. Keep that in mind if you book a similar tour. The headphone-guided tours take longer than necessary. Either do without them, listen at some stops rather than all of them, or get an actual guide person.

The head of the goddess *Sulis Minerva*

I was so traumatized by the cold in London that I couldn't do any more activities. I decided,

"F*@# this sh*t."

I decided to fly south for warmth, like the birds, and head to Rome. After that I would fly back to London via Amsterdam so I could spend a day in the Netherlands. Luckily, budget airlines make traveling around Europe purse friendly.

I left my suitcase at the hotel and traveled only with my backpack. I booked a hotel near the Colosseum in Rome, and I was good to go.

Italy

The Colosseum in Rome

The Colosseum was the main reason I went to Rome. My fifth grade history teacher instilled in me a love of the history of ancient civilizations, including Roman history. I find museums stale, but I really enjoy visiting historical sites and learning more about their historical significance. I couldn't wait to see the famous Colosseum in person.

I had only budgeted one day in Rome. I figured that would give me enough time to see the Colosseum. I arrived at Leonardo da Vinci Fiumicino Airport in the early afternoon. As usual, I took a cab to my hotel. Time was of the essence and I could not afford the time to take trains and figure out how to get to my hotel from the station.

Traffic in Rome seemed chaotic but worked with minimal honking. Cars drove on the right. The city seemed older and quainter than London.

FROM ANTARCTICA TO ZIMBABWE

As soon as I checked in to my hotel, I headed out to the Colosseum, which was only a 5 minute walk away. The receptionist at the hotel had warned me that they closed at sundown, which was around 5 pm. Unfortunately, it was rainy so the Colosseum closed at 3:30 pm that day, right before I got there. I was so disappointed since that was the main reason I was in Rome. I considered my options. The Colosseum opened at 8:30 am. My flight to Amsterdam left at 10 the following morning. It would take at least 30 minutes to get to the airport, so returning to the Colosseum in the morning before my flight was not an option. I realized I would just have to come back to Rome someday. I walked around the perimeter enjoying the view. I chatted with one of the guides and he gave me a brief history of the Colosseum. I recalled some of it from my fifth grade history class.

The Colosseum, or Coliseum, is an amphitheater built from stone and concrete. Building started around 72 A.D. by the Roman Emperor Vespasian and was completed by his son and successor Titus around 80 A.D. It could hold over 50,000 spectators. Events held there included chariot races and gladiator fights.

As I walked around the Colosseum, I met a priest from Zimbabwe who was in town attending a conference. We chatted about life and such, and I explained that I was traveling around the world. He couldn't understand why I was traveling when I should be looking for a job. I tried to explain and he eventually seemed to get it. Knowing that Zimbabwe was on my itinerary, he asked me to give him a call when I arrived in the country. I said I would try.

I decided to take a tour of Rome. I took the Hop On Hop Off bus and went all around Rome. By the time we returned to the Colosseum, it was dark. I walked back to my hotel, taking note of the police cars around the amphitheater.

I was stopped by a young man named Antonio who asked if I would join him for dinner. Having had nothing to eat all day, I was ravenous but also irritable and cold. I told him I was married and not interested. He asked if I was separated or divorced. I told him no. He said,

> "There's a saying we have: What happens in Rome stays in Rome."

I had to laugh at the audacity. He paid me many compliments which was, I must admit, good for my ego but I couldn't understand why he felt he had to try so hard. He wasn't bad looking but I could smell the desperation on him. Surely he should have no issues finding a nice girl to date.

Antonio took me to the top of the stairs where we could see the Colosseum lit up in all its glory. It was really beautiful at night.

> "Isn't it romantic?"

he asked, putting his arm around me.

At that point, the dregs of my patience fizzled out, exposing my last nerve. I said sternly,

> "Look, I'm cold and hungry. I have to go...."

I shrugged his arm off and made my way back to my hotel. It's my personal policy not to be out at night by myself in unfamiliar places but night had come quicker than I had anticipated. I was glad to note that there were a few people nearby, and of course, the police. I looked back often to make sure Antonio was not following me.

When I was far enough away from Antonio, I started

looking for suitable places to eat. I had had nothing to eat all day and I was starving. I found a pleasant looking place, and ordered a pizza, although I'm not a fan of cheese. It was thin crust and very delicious. Even though I was stuffed, when the waiter recommended the tiramisu for dessert, I ordered it. I topped everything off with a latte. I learned from this experience that when traveling, one should eat whenever the opportunity presents itself because otherwise you don't know when your next meal will be.

Graffiti in Rome

After dinner, I strolled back to my hotel, enjoying watching the people around me. I stopped to window shop at boutiques along the way. The clothes were really unique and I would have loved to buy some but I just knew I had no extra space in my suitcase. I resisted the urge and kept walking. I saw some creative graffiti along the way. When I got tired of walking, I turned around and made my way back to my hotel room, which was even smaller than my London hotel room. After a nice, hot shower, I fell soundly asleep.

In the morning, I took the express train from Roma terminal to Fiumicino Airport. I had to ask directions from the police a couple times. Without realizing it, I had picked a really good location in my hotel. It was near the metro, near the Colosseum, and one stop from the Fiumicino express, which went to the Fiumicino Airport. It was all very convenient.

My general opinion of Italians is that they were pleasant and friendly. I really liked the feel of Rome and I plan to return when I can. I also plan to do a lot of shopping when I do. My experience with Antonio has given me a not so favorable opinion of Italian men but I reserve judgment since I was there for such a short time.

The Netherlands

Head sculptures in Amsterdam

Upon arrival in Amsterdam from Rome, I was amazed to see there was no immigration check. I wish it was always this easy to travel. I only had about eight hours in Amsterdam so I was determined to maximize my day. After talking with the people at the tourist counter, I decided to take a canal tour of the city, then maybe visit the Ann Frank museum. I had been to the one in Atlanta and found it very moving. I was curious how the one in Amsterdam would compare.

Buying a train ticket at the airport was a pain as the machine would not accept my credit card. I ended up having to use my debit card. I took the train from Schiphol Airport to Amsterdam Centraal station, which took around twenty minutes. Across from the station, I found a canal cruise company, paid for my ticket and settled down in the boat.

The boat cruised along the canals around the city. The tour was given in both English and Chinese, as there were several Chinese tourists on board.

As usual, I was hijacked by Chinese tourists who took a lot of pictures of me, and with me. I say as usual because this happens to me often when I travel. The most intense was on Phi Phi Island where for almost an hour after landing, I moved from group to group of Chinese tourists, posing and carrying babies. Sometimes, they simply took selfies as I passed by. The tourists on the boat were very friendly and spoke some English. We chatted and they told me about China, encouraging me to visit. I still haven't figured out why they are so fascinated with me.

There is a one hour time difference between Amsterdam and London, and the flight was only 45 minutes long. I arrived in London before I left. As I walked to my hotel, I noted that the weather was still crappy but much warmer than in Amsterdam. Still, the English tradition of drinking tea finally made sense. It's obviously done to combat the cold. I had never thought about it before.

London is a very busy city. Walking or trying to walk through Victoria Station at rush hour is an experience. There are so many people going briskly in every direction. It's best to avoid it until rush hour is over. Dodging numerous buses as I tried to make my way to my hotel was also scary and not for the faint of heart.

The following day was my last full day in London. I decided to take it easy and get my strength back. My next destination was Casablanca, but I decided that I had to go to Marrakech and the Sahara as well. That meant I would be in Morocco for about a week instead of just a couple days. Therefore I had to adjust some of the flights that came after Morocco. I planned out all the changes, then called AirTreks, paid a fee and the changes were made. I was impressed by the efficiency of the travel agency and very glad I booked with them.

The next morning, I visited Buckingham Palace before I left for the airport. Note that you cannot go through the gates to the palace so, along with other tourists, I stood at the gate and took pictures. Fluffy and I took pictures of the gates, and the sculptures outside the palace. I was lucky to catch the changing of the Queen's Guard while I was there.

The changing of the guard outside Buckingham Palace

I returned to the hotel and ordered a cab to Heathrow Airport. It was cheaper than my cab from Gatwick. I had an interesting time with Heathrow security. I had more than one bag of liquids over 100 ml. They flagged my suitcase and removed everything from it, with particular emphasis on the liquids. They swabbed my bag and the liquids and tested them. There was a positive reaction but they didn't know where it came from. They tested the suitcase by itself and the test was negative. They tested all the liquids and those came back positive. I was just as surprised as they were. Then they tested the liquids one by one. My insect repellent was the culprit. I probably shouldn't have been surprised since the stuff works like a charm, better than anything else I've ever used. I never get bitten when I use it. It's called Passport Health Controlled Release Insect Repellent. Anyway, they let me keep it but they only let me take what liquids could fit into one bag.

As I repacked my bag, I was chatting with the security guy and explaining my trip to him. It turned out that his daughter is a medical student who would shortly be traveling to a village in Zambia, one of my destinations. She was going to build houses and help at an AIDS hospice. He asked if it was safe there and I put his mind at ease. Because of the many years I spent there, I could tell him that Zambia is a very safe, very chill country. Zambians are very friendly and laid back. I told him to make sure she visited the magnificent Victoria Falls, also called Mosi-oa-Tunya Falls.

At Heathrow, gates are not announced until roughly 30 minutes before the flight. It was a little unnerving but I had to sit around and wait until the gate was announced.

Tips for travel to Europe

- For public transit, ask when the train or bus starts and stops running.

- If traveling to Europe in winter, dress more warmly than you think you should especially if traveling to northern Europe.

- Get an International Driver's license if you plan to drive.

- Pack light so you don't have to pay extra fees on discount airlines. It also makes staying in small hotel rooms, which are the norm in Europe, easier.

- Don't pack too many liquids.

- Learning self-defense skills can help you protect yourself if unexpected things happen.

- Budget airlines allow for quick and cheap travel between countries in Europe.

CHAPTER 4
AFRICA

FROM ANTARCTICA TO ZIMBABWE

The flight to Casablanca was at least half empty. I had an entire row to myself on the B737-800. The 4 hour flight was uneventful and we arrived in Casablanca around 8:30 pm. Going through immigration, I noticed a picture of King Mohammed VI of Morocco and I was struck by how handsome he was. Heads of state are not usually so pleasant-looking. The immigration agent was even friendlier than the ones in London.

Stepping foot in Africa is always awesome, because it's home for me. I had never been to North Africa before but I felt right at home. I was reminded of the late Miriam Makeba's words, upon her return to South Africa after 30 years of exile:

> "I'm so happy to be back home, I can't tell you."

Africa is a huge continent, second only to Asia in area, comprising 54 different countries. More than 2,000 languages are spoken on the continent. Most countries have over 100 distinct languages. As a result, most Africans are multilingual. The hallmark of Africa is hospitality even to its own detriment. We always treat visitors better than we treat ourselves.

Morocco

Having tea with a nomad Berber family in the Sahara Desert

The official languages of Morocco are Arabic and Berber. French is the unofficial third language. Knowing a decent amount of French had served me well in Argentina and Rome since French and Spanish are somewhat similar. I was looking forward to dabbling in French for a change.

My experiences in Europe, while pleasant overall, had left me feeling quite disconnected from the average person. The cold had really kept me inside my shell. Now that I was warm again, I was yearning to live more like locals, and less like a tourist.

On my way to find a cab at the airport, I noticed a young lady who was there to pick up a passenger. I loved her braids and I went over to her and told her. Her regal bearing reminded me of Ngozi, a good friend of mine whom I was missing terribly at that moment. I spoke to her in French, and found out she was from Senegal and she was there to pick up her fiancé who was arriving from Paris. When I asked for directions to the cab stand, she hesitated then told me she would have her brother take me to my hotel. It was my turn to hesitate. On the one hand, this would allow me to quickly learn a lot about Morocco, at least from their point of view. On the other hand, I didn't know these people and anything could happen. I decided to take a chance.

Sometimes you take a leap and things work out better than you could have imagined. This was not one of those times. The young lady's brother, let's call him David, helped me carry my bag, while the sister, Nefer, remained behind waiting on her fiancée. The agreement was I would pay him for his trouble but less than what I would pay a regular cab. As we drove away from the airport, I noticed Christmas lights and decorations lining the street. Knowing that the main religion in Morocco is Islam, this suggested a great degree of tolerance.

After ten minutes, David received a phone call. He spoke into the phone in Wolof, a Senegalese language. Without saying a word to me, he turned around and headed back to the airport.

"Qu'est-ce qui c'est passe? What's going on?"

I asked.

"Oh, I have to go back and get my sister."

Now, I'm an engineer for a reason. I abhor inefficiency. So, unsurprisingly, I was starting to get irritated at this point. Why leave the airport only to turn around again? Why not let me know what was happening? I should have gone to find a proper cab at that point, but I decided to be patient and see how things turned out. I didn't feel like I was in any danger so I wasn't worried, just annoyed.

After we picked up Nefer and her fiancée, we again made our way to Casablanca, which was about 40 minutes away. Once we arrived, David had a lot of trouble finding my hotel even though I had the address. We stopped for directions many times but somehow he just couldn't find the hotel. We drove around for 45 minutes and finally stopped at a hotel he believed to be the right one. Now, the name was slightly different so I knew it wasn't the right place but I just wanted to get away from him at this point. Inside the hotel, we discovered that this was indeed the wrong hotel. I asked the concierge to call me a cab but David pleaded and begged me to come back with him. Once again, I gave him the benefit of the doubt. Thirty minutes later, we were still searching for my hotel. I had him stop at the next hotel we saw and I had them call me a cab. David tried begging again for me to get back in his car. I'm not sure why it was so important to him but I was tired and fed up so I sternly told him,

"Non! Ça suffit! That's enough!"

But I was really thinking

"F*@# this sh*t."

The concierge couldn't understand why I was so angry. He tried to persuade me to go with David as my hotel was apparently less than 5 minutes away. I had to explain to him that we had been 5 minutes away for over an hour. I gave David some money and he left. My cab arrived and it probably took 2 minutes for us to get to my hotel. Lesson learned and I take full responsibility for my actions. If you want something done right, use a professional. At least I got a story out of the whole experience.

My hotel room was huge, especially compared to the hotel rooms in Europe. It had a hallway, kitchenette and living room, in addition to the bathroom. I noticed my hotel room smelled like incense and I would smell this scent all over Morocco in the days to come. In fact, I later saw a cab driver spray his cab with the smell of incense.

I FaceTimed with Hubby, but left out the story of my adventure with David. I was too ashamed to share it with him or anyone else. In retrospect, this is the dumbest thing I've ever done while traveling. I don't recommend it. The whole Taken franchise is based on this premise.

When I was in my mid-teens, I had to travel from Zambia to Cameroon by myself for school. The trip involved transit through Nairobi. I had done the trip with my dad so I was at least familiar with all the airports and processes involved. As I was sitting at Jomo Kenyatta Airport in Nairobi, I was approached by an older man. He said he was from Pakistan and he was looking for a wife for his son, i.e. me. I told him I was headed someplace and I had deadlines. He told me to come with them just to see if I liked Pakistan, and they would pay for me to travel on to Cameroon after that. He pointed out his son who was sitting and watching us. Even at that age, I thought what was happening was bizarre. Now, I was born for adventure, and I liked the thought of traveling to Pakistan just to check it out. But I remembered my dad's very stern warnings not to talk to anyone and I knew he would kill me for even entertaining these people. I told the man very politely that I wasn't interested. He came back a couple more times, once with his son, and literally begged me to go with them. I turned him down every time. I don't know what would have happened to me but I might still be in Pakistan today if I had gone with them. I've never told my dad this story either.

In the morning, I partook of the free breakfast provided by

the hotel. My favorite item was the omelette which was made with tomatoes, onions and some incredible-tasting spices. Afterwards, I returned to my room to plan my itinerary. It had been a dream of mine for several years to visit the Sahara Desert. I visited a local travel agency a fifteen minute walk from the hotel. Walking in Casablanca is an adventure. Traffic lights are positioned so that pedestrians at the stop cannot see them. There was a lot of traffic, so crossing the street was very invigorating.

Casablanca is the financial hub of Morocco so there isn't much to do for tourists. I noticed that covering is optional for women. It was bright and sunny with temperatures around 55°F.

I made it to the travel agency in one piece. We talked possibilities but the prices they quoted were astronomical, partly because I would be leaving from Casablanca. From talking with them, though, I got options for how to get to the Sahara: you could fly from Casablanca to Ouarzazate, then drive to Merzouga and launch into the desert from there, or you could drive from either Casablanca or Marrakech to Merzouga. The travel agent told me I would love the Sahara but I was disappointed to find out she had never been herself.

I was dying to see Marrakech so I decided to go there first. Some internet searches gave me many tour companies that would get me from Marrakech to Merzouga by road, then into the desert. I booked a tour with a company that had great reviews. Rather than fly to Marrakech, I decided to take the train so I could enjoy the landscapes and interact with people.

The train left from Casa Voyageurs station and took three and a half hours to get to Marrakech. It was comfortable in the very reasonably priced first class cabin I booked. My companions were friendly and we chatted a little. The older couple in the cabin shared their food with the rest of us. The tall, strapping middle-aged man brought everyone's luggage down when we arrived in Marrakech. Moroccans are truly the nicest people I've ever met.

Mint tea I was welcomed with in Marrakech

Upon arrival in Marrakech, around 3 pm, I noticed it was much warmer than Casablanca. It was easily around 75°F and I was forced to remove layers until I was down to my t-shirt. I was picked up by Khalid, a tour guide from the tour company. He was very pleasant and we were joking and laughing within minutes of meeting each other. He gave me a brief driving tour of the city. He explained that an international film festival was taking place in Marrakech at that time. This was the first time I heard that Morocco is big in the movie industry.

Khalid drove me to my hotel in the old walled city or medina. The hotels in the medina are riads, i.e. traditional houses with gardens in the interior. The alleys leading to the riads are so narrow that vehicles cannot fit through them. Khalid had to call my riad and they sent someone to come out and help with my luggage. We parted ways and he left me with this warning,

> "Beware of pickpockets. And be careful of the motorcycles."

There were so many twists and turns leading to my riad that I was convinced I could never leave it on my own or I would surely get lost. We arrived and I was immediately welcomed with absinthe tea. The garden in my riad was very picturesque. I even saw birds flitting around the fountains. My room was very quaint. I could not stop marveling at how picturesque everything was. I had delicious fish tagine for a late lunch then I left the riad to explore. I walked to the Place Jemaa el Fna looking out for motorcycles. I quickly realized why Khalid had warned me about them. They would appear out of nowhere, traveling the wrong way on pavements, endangering oblivious pedestrians. I made sure to look in every possible direction before crossing the street.

Keeping in mind Khalid's warning about pickpockets, I had left my passport and purse behind and only carried a small amount of money.

The Place Jemaa el Fna is the biggest square in Marrakech. There you can find vendors selling anything you can imagine from spices to cooked food to clothes and jewelry. In the evenings, the entertainers come out singing songs, playing instruments, telling stories, performing magic, etc. The square is very crowded especially in the evenings, and I enjoyed the hustle and bustle of life happening around me. I stopped at one and tried on some clothing and a turban. I bought a beautiful green ring from the vendor and that ate up most of my cash. The vendor warned me not to eat any of the food sold at the square or I might have stomach issues.

Trying on new threads at the Place Jemaa el Fna

As I wandered around, I was approached by a woman selling henna. I turned her down, telling her truthfully that I didn't have enough money to pay for henna. She insisted on giving me just a test design. As the test design got bigger and bigger, I reminded her that I had no money and tried to take my arm away. She told me it was no problem but continued. After she was done, she threw glitter at the henna. Then she held her hand out and asked for payment. I shook my head sternly and reminded her that I had warned her I had no money. Be careful if you visit the Place. Anything offered for free probably is not. I walked away from her promising I would visit her again next time I came to the square. Unfortunately, I never got a chance to return to the Place so I never did see her again.

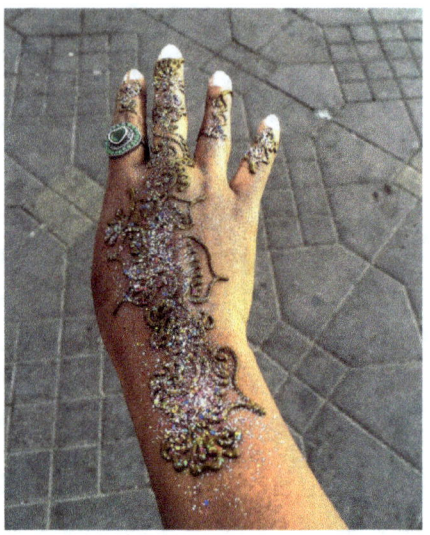

Henna design with glitter

It was getting dark and I couldn't do much with my hand and arm covered in henna so I started making my way back to the riad. I knew it would be tricky to find during the day let alone at night. My excellent sense of direction got me there but it was well and truly dark by then. The door was shut and I had to ring the bell to be let in. I reflected on my day and decided that Marrakech was the epitome of exotic.

Khalid picked me up from the riad very early the next morning. Our itinerary was Marrakech to Aït Ben Haddou, Ouarzazate, the Valley of Roses, Dades Gorge, then Merzouga at the edge of the Sahara. The drive from Marrakech was beautiful. Morocco is full of beautiful landscapes and is a photographer's dream.

My riad in the medina in Marrakech

It was chilly that morning and as we drove out of Marrakech and through the Atlas Mountains, the temperature dropped as low as 45°F. Fortunately, it warmed up once the sun came out. Morocco has wonderful highways which make exploring the country easy. I always consider roads through mountains feats of engineering and they are well done in Morocco.

One of our first stops was the famous Ksar Aït Ben Haddou. A ksar is a group of clay buildings surrounded by a high wall. Historically, the ksar was a safe place for caravans to spend the night.

Aït Ben Haddou has been used as the site for many movies including Lawrence of Arabia, The Mummy, Prince of Persia: The Sands of Time, Gladiator, Raiders of the Lost Ark, and the popular television show, Game of Thrones.

Fluffums and I in front of the Ksar Aït Ben Haddou

After we left the ksar, we drove on to Ouarzazate, the quiet city. It is considered the gateway to the Sahara and is popular with movie makers. We visited a movie studio then got back on the road, heading to the Valley of Roses.

During the drive, Khalid and I chatted about life in general. He had some awesome sayings including,

> "When you are tranquil, life comes to you. When you are stressed, life goes from you."

That one really hit home. I was enjoying my trip around the world so much. However, occasionally thoughts of the future would creep into my mind and disrupt my fun. I was determined to enjoy myself and worry when the trip was over. Putting my mind at ease would help me figure out what I wanted to do with my life.

We drove through the Skoura Valley, which is famous as a site for growing dates. Of course we stopped at the side of the road and bought some. They were sweet and delicious and we snacked on them as we drove. We drove on to the Valley of Roses and arrived in the early evening. The Valley of Roses is known, of course, for its massive rose industry. Roses are grown and sold as-is, or the oil is extracted and used in cosmetics and other products. Rose water is supposed to be good for preventing crow's feet and other wrinkles. We arrived too late to visit a factory where extraction occurs so we stopped at a cosmetic store instead.

Our last stop for the night was in Boulmane Dadès where Khalid had arranged for us to have tea with a semi-nomadic Berber family. Nomadic Berbers are always on the move, looking for vegetation for their animals. Semi-nomadic families have two homes; they live in the valley in the winter and move to the mountains in the summer, again so that their animals can feed. The family we joined for tea was like all the other Moroccans I had come in contact with, very nice and hospitable people. They showed us around their compound and I saw where they kept their sheep and cows, and the well they pulled water from. The evening was chilly so I was grateful for the tea and almonds they offered us. As soon as I sipped the tea, I could feel my whole body warming up. In the winter, absinthe tea is drunk to warm up the body, and I can confirm, it works very well. In the summer, mint tea is drunk to cool the body.

After some time, we bade the family goodbye and headed to our hotel.

Windy road through the Dadès Gorge

After a big breakfast the following morning, we headed out to Dadès Gorge stopping along the way at a rock formation called the Pattes de Singe, or feet of a monkey. The rocks really do look like the bottom of a monkey's feet. It occurred to me that my geologist friends would love visiting Morocco.

Our next stop was the Todgha Valley which is a river oasis. The green of the plants, the brown of the kasbahs, the purple of the mountains and the blue of the sky provided such perfect contrast to each other, I could have stood watching them for hours. A kasbah is a clay house. Kasbahs are built ecologically. They are built into cliffsides from clay and straw to make them waterproof. Every 3 years or so, the walls are re-mudded. Disused houses easily return to nature.

The Todgha Valley

The drive was very scenic, the blue of the sky contrasting beautifully with the red of the mountains, the occasional kasbahs and valleys providing even more eye candy. I would have been happy just driving for days and soaking up the scenery.

We often saw signs for argan oil for sale. Argan oil is processed in Morocco from the nut of the argan tree. The government has set up argan oil cooperatives primarily for widows and divorced women. The women get startup money from the government, which allows them to set up the business and become self-sufficient.

Dadès Gorge

We drove on to the Dadès Gorge winding through the mountains and enjoying the view of the valley. I spent some time admiring the massive stone walls on either side of the water, marveling at the power of water to forge a path through solid rock.

We next stopped at a qanat, an irrigation system which comprises a system of vertical shafts hand-dug into a sloping channel pulling from an underground aquifer. This amazing technology was developed in the first millennium

B.C. in Persia. I went down into the qanat and walked through the channel, looking up at the vertical shafts along the way.

After the tour of the qanat, we stopped at a shop where fossils from the Sahara Desert are processed and sold. I was awed by the size of some of them. Apparently, they are so plentiful that whole pieces of furniture are made out of rocks containing numerous fossils. Individual fossils are also available. The fossils are mostly from the triassic, jurassic and cretaceous periods. Once again, I thought of my geologist friends and how much they would love Morocco.

After the fossil shop, we headed for Merzouga. We drove through the Stony Sahara which is flat and, as the name implies, full of stones. The Atlas Mountains were on one side, the Anti-Atlas Mountains on the other side, and the dunes of the Sandy Sahara were in front of us. I was overwhelmed by all the beauty around us.

We arrived at our hotel in Merzouga late in the evening. I left most of my luggage at the hotel and left for the Sahara with a new guide and a camel to camp overnight. My dream was about to come true and I thought my heart would burst from beating so fast. I rode and my guide, Omar, led the camel. This part of the Sahara Desert near Merzouga is called Erg Chebbi. The camel ride through the dunes lasted for about an hour before we got to the camp site. We stopped on the dunes to watch the sun set. It was sublime and surreal. I was so happy that I couldn't stop smiling.

When we arrived at the camp, there were other tourists already there. A couple from Houston also working in the oil and gas industry, a couple from southern Spain, and 2 other guides. There were 4 Berber tents set up for sleeping, and a bigger tent where we ate. The night sky was filled with stars until the bright, full moon came out and dimmed their sparkle.

As we ate dinner, Eva, the girl from Spain, expressed her doubts that anyone could travel around the world in three months. Europeans have up to six weeks of vacation time on average. Usually, when I run into them on my travels, they are spending one month at a time in one place. Things are very different in the US where two weeks' vacation is standard. By this time, I had become skilled at maximizing my vacation time. One week is more than enough to spend in any one country. That's enough time to travel to at least three different cities and get a good feel for a country. There may be some exceptions where ten days or two weeks would be better. Still, I would get bored anywhere if I was there for a whole month.

What stuck with me the most though, was another lady who was with her husband. She declared that she would never travel on her own. I looked around and told her,

> "But you and I are here, and nothing bad has happened to us."

She simply shook her head, and I shrugged. People choose to limit themselves. I couldn't force her to be more adventurous.

After dinner, we all sat around a fire outside, while the guides played drums and sang. It was cold that night especially once the sun set, so we were very grateful for the heat of the fire. The guides spoke many languages: Berber, Arabic, English, French, Portuguese, Spanish, and German. This comes in handy when they deal with tourists from all around the world. It helped that night as the Spanish couple only spoke a little English and I spoke very little Spanish.

Around midnight, we turned in. I had a tent to myself and was thrilled to find 6 blankets on my bed. Khalid had warned Omar that I get cold very easily. In spite of all the blankets, I was still cold and it took a long time for me to get warm. I woke up in the middle of the night with a hacking cough. It felt like I had sand in my lungs. I finally understood the need for face coverings in the desert.

Desert camp at sunrise

I needed to use the toilet but I dreaded trudging through the sand in my boots. It was really difficult to walk in the sand with them. I started to walk in my socks to the shack that housed the toilet and regretted it immediately. The camels had pooped all over the area and I could feel their round poop pellets under my feet. I did my business and returned to my tent. It took another half hour before I fell asleep again.

In the morning, we climbed to the top of the nearest dune and watched the sun rise. The dunes stretched for miles around us. The rising sun turned the sky purple and lit up the pink and orange dunes until I almost couldn't bear the beauty in front of me.

Later that morning, Omar and the camel and I bade everyone farewell and headed back to my hotel in Merzouga. My camel was nicknamed Omar II; the others were called Jimmy Hendrix and Bob Marley. I had enjoyed the overnight stay in the Sahara but it felt too brief. On the way back, my ears were assaulted by the sound of ATVs. It sounded wrong. The beauty of the Sahara, besides the dunes and the colors, is the quiet. The ATVs completely interrupted that part of it and I was annoyed.

It was around 8 am by the time we got back to the hotel. Khalid wanted to know if I enjoyed myself. I explained that while I had had a great time, I needed more time in the desert. The plan was for us to head back to Marrakech that day but after one look at my face, Khalid suggested we stay an extra day and he would take me back into the desert. I jumped for joy and agreed.

After a shower and big breakfast, I joined Khalid in the car and we headed out for the day. We spent some time with the Gnaoua people, listening to them play their spiritual music. They are descended from the northern part of West Africa. They served us tea and almonds while they played. I joined them for a little while and played the finger cymbals. I was most struck by their somber demeanor. It suggested that their music is not for entertainment but for a spiritual purpose.

We drove into the desert and came upon a nomad Berber family. The mother was weaving cloth at a loom with her two children close by. The husband was away with the animals. She welcomed us and served us tea, bread and almonds. I've never drunk as much tea in my life as I did when I was in Morocco. I was able to leave England without drinking a single cup of tea but that would have been impossible in Morocco. It would have been impolite to decline, as it would be in most African cultures, so I thanked her and drank and ate.

Riding camels in the Sahara Desert

The children were adorable and very shy. They clung to their mother but peeked at us from the folds of her dress. We brought out some fruit from the car and they lost all shyness immediately and ran to us. I realized that fruit must be scarce in the desert so it had to be like candy for the children. When we left, I thought about how I had learned about the Berbers in my social studies classes. I could hardly believe I was living so many things I had only read about.

We drove along a dry river bed and stopped at a beautiful set of dunes. We walked along the dunes then stopped at a spot that had a good view. We sat on the dune for almost an hour, not speaking, just enjoying the quiet. The quiet led to introspection and I allowed myself to finally deal with everything that had happened with my job: the stress, the disappointment, the anger, the hurt. I allowed myself to feel all of it so I could deal with it and move on. Most of all, I needed to forgive myself for staying at the job when I hated it so much. I did it for the money which was the best decision in the long run, but I vowed not to allow myself to stay in a situation like that again. This was the most cathartic moment of my trip and I felt like a new person after that. Khalid reminded me,

> "Relax. Life will come to you."

I really felt at home in the desert. Maybe I was a nomad in my past life. I vowed to return so I could do yoga in the Sahara. It was winter so it never got too hot on the dunes. Even in the middle of the day, it didn't get warmer than 60°F and when the wind blew, it blew cold. The best way to climb a dune is barefoot but that would be difficult in the summer when the sand is burning hot.

We headed out of the desert in a pleasant silence, my mind cleared and my soul purified. Then without warning, we got stuck in the sand. First I'm on a ship that hits an iceberg, and now this. Khalid had never gotten stuck in the sand before and he had been guiding for over a decade. Maybe my being there had something to do with all these things happening. Curiously, I didn't feel stressed or worried at all. Whatever happened, I knew we would figure a way out.

Meditating in the Sahara

We got out and tried to clear the sand away from the stuck tire but we could not get the SUV clear. After forty five minutes, I looked up and saw a young man coming towards us. He jumped in and started helping us. About ten minutes later, an older guy showed up and pitched in as well. They had been walking by and noticed our car wasn't moving, so they came over to make sure we were okay. We ended up calling a tow vehicle to pull us out, and flattening our tires so we wouldn't get stuck again.

Khalid was Berber and he explained to me that the symbol of the Berber people is their letter yaz, or Z, and looks like this: ⵣ. It symbolizes a free man, and therefore, freedom from oppression. I really liked the idea of a symbol that represents freedom. With all the positive experiences I had had in Morocco, I decided that a necklace with the yaz would remind me to protect my own freedom. I bought one from a vendor on the side of the road on the way back to Marrakech. I still wear it to remind myself to stay free.

I learned a few Arabic words and showed them off every chance I got:

> *Shoukran.* Thank you
> *Bismillah.* In the name of God
> *Inshallah.* If God wills it
> *Lebez.* I'm fine

Every time I was able to respond in Arabic, I was rewarded with delighted smiles. People were genuinely pleased that I tried to learn their language. *Inshallah* was used often. For instance, whenever we parted ways with someone, they would ask us to stay longer. I would tell them that I would be back. They would respond with *Inshallah*.

Khalid told me of a Berber named Ibn Battuta from the 1300s who traveled almost all over the world. He is quoted as saying,

> "Traveling - it leaves you speechless and then turns you into a storyteller."

What a perfect way to describe traveling. I was certainly lost for words in Morocco but I knew I would be sharing these stories with my friends the first chance I got. I was also moved by a quote from Khalid himself,

> "A tourist goes to see nature. A traveler goes to see life."

We returned to the hotel in Merzouga just as the sun was

setting. I watched in awe from the terrace as the sun kissed the tops of the dunes. That night we had camel tagine for dinner with eggs. This dish is special to the Merzouga region and was made courtesy of the inn keeper. We chatted with him while we ate. He talked about how things are changing for better and worse. The internet allows us to connect across the globe. However, it is changing the tradition where people come together in the evenings to talk. Now when you find a group, they're usually all on their phones and not talking to each other.

After dinner, we sat around chatting for a while even though we were exhausted. Khalid told me a story that I'd like to share.

> "There was once a beautiful elephant that lived in a beautiful forest that few people knew about. One day, a hunter discovered the forest, then the elephant. He was so blown away by the beauty of the elephant that he went back home and told everyone he knew about it. Soon, more and more people arrived at the forest to see the beautiful elephant. Eventually, one man came and took the elephant away and put it in a zoo so that many more people could see it. The elephant tried to escape many times and finally the man chained a metal ball to its foot. The ball was so heavy that the elephant could barely move and after trying for a long time, it finally stopped trying to escape. After many years, the man replaced the metal ball with a wooden ball. By this time, the elephant was so conditioned to not being able to escape that it didn't even try to move the wooden ball. Eventually, the elephant died in the zoo."

The story made me really sad. The moral of the story is simple. We have perceived limitations on ourselves. If we would only try, we would surprise ourselves with what is

possible. Another way Khalid put it,

> "We see the dunes and we worry about what is behind them. But when we get to the top, we see that there's nothing there to be afraid of."

We chatted for a while. When I could absorb no more wisdom, I went to the terrace to look up at the stars then I went to bed. I was at great peace that night. I felt like I had achieved what I came to Morocco for, and more.

The next morning, we were up bright and early since we had a full day's drive ahead of us to get back to Marrakech. The innkeeper gave us a huge breakfast and we bade him a fond farewell. We made a quick stop so I could taste fresh camel's milk. It tasted the same as cow's milk except that it was noticeably saltier. We watched the milking process. First the baby camel is brought to its mother, without which she will not produce milk. They are kept apart so that the baby doesn't drink up all the milk. One of the mother's knees is tied so she doesn't walk away. After milking is over, the milk is filtered and then drunk. It was still warm when I drank it. It's supposed to be good for dealing with the desert environment.

Khalid was an excellent guide. He talked to everyone as if they were an old friend. We found out a lot of information this way. He explained that nomads are not afraid to talk to people and ask for what they want no matter where they find themselves. This certainly worked out well for us. He is the best guide I have ever had, and I have had tours literally all over the world. The guide makes or breaks the experience.

We drove back to Marrakech, taking a different route which took us through the Anti-Atlas Mountains. The drive was pleasant and the scenery spectacular as always. We saw Berber women dressed in very colorful clothing while Bedouin women covered their faces and wore black clothing. We listened to music as we drove and I gained some new favorites: "From Medina" by Birahim; "Zawali" by DJMawi Africa; and "Love Story" by Indila. Till this day, the minute I hear any of these songs, I am transported back to that SUV going through the mountains with the desert all around us.

That afternoon, we were driving and singing along to "Lovely Day" by Bill Withers when the car started overheating. Fortunately, we were only ten minutes outside of Ouarzazate. As soon as we pulled off the road, a truck driver stopped to see if we needed help. Khalid was talking to him when yet another trucker stopped to help us. I love Morocco. The truckers gave us a gallon of water. We had to pull further off the road so more people wouldn't stop. Khalid was amazed because the car had never had any issues. It must have been me again.

We called a mechanic and he diagnosed the problem over the phone: the engine had overheated because the water pump had failed. The mechanic found a replacement pump and drove out to us. I had the option to take another car and driver and return to Marrakech. I decided to stay and see the adventure to the end. The mechanic successfully fixed the car and three hours after we broke down, we were back on the road.

Our adventures were not over. Right after heading out again, we were speeding and we got pulled over by the police, even though we had been warned by oncoming motorists. They were very nice though. I exchanged personal information with one of them and flirted hard with him. He offered to send camels to my husband so I could stay with him in Morocco. Khalid worked his own angle of having no money left to pay fines after paying for repairs. Something clicked and we were allowed to leave without paying the fine.

By then it was almost 5 pm and we were still roughly 4 hours away from Marrakech. We stopped at a small town along the way for dinner. We picked out a cut of beef we wanted and it was cut up and grilled for us. Of course the meal started with tea. After dinner, we continued on our way, giving an old man a ride home. It had started raining by then and Khalid, even though he didn't personally know the old man, didn't want him to walk home through the rain and cold. This is the African way.

I felt bad for Khalid. We were driving through the rain around curves in the mountains. I was exhausted so I could only imagine how he felt. I dozed until we finally arrived in Marrakech around 10 pm. I didn't have a hotel reservation so Khalid and his roommate kindly let me stay with them. Saïd, the roommate, asked me my favorite Moroccan breakfast and dinner dishes. I told him I really liked Berber omelettes and tagine.

They disappeared into the kitchen while I got settled. I went looking for them and found that they were making beef tagine. I felt terrible for inconveniencing them but they insisted on making dinner. I couldn't believe how delicious the food was. It was the best food I had during my entire stay in Morocco. I had a delicious orange for dessert. Apparently, Morocco grows some of the best oranges in the world. We ate at midnight then watched TV for a while.

CNN news was on and the anchors were discussing a shooting in California. Khalid and Saïd could not understand why I was on my phone and not paying attention. I tried to explain that this happens all the time in the US. You're sad for a minute then you get on with your life. You have to because there is a shooting practically every day. They thought it was good this happened because maybe now people would be forced to make changes. I tried to explain that some people in the US see the solution differently. The spectrum of suggested solutions runs from no guns to everyone having guns. Understandably they were shocked. I reassured them that somehow, most of us manage to escape being shot every day. If they decided to visit, I would be happy to show them the same hospitality they had shown me. We finally went to bed and I slept like a baby.

They made a Berber omelette for breakfast. We sat around and ate with our hands from the same pan using bread to pick up the omelette. It quickly became clear that I was not pulling my weight.

"Eat!"

Khalid kept telling me. I'd be lucky to get out of Morocco with only five pounds of extra weight. I turned to his roommate Saïd.

"He's so bossy,"

I said. Saïd laughed and nodded. Then he said,

"Eat!"

I sighed but I ate it all. After I finished my coffee, Saïd poured me a glass of tea. I obediently drank it all, but I felt like I would never be hungry again.

It was warm in Marrakech, around 70°F. We went to the train station and bought a ticket to Casablanca. The train didn't leave for a few hours so we went to a cafe and drank tea and hot chocolate. I reflected on the trip and posted pictures to Instagram.

A street in Marrakech

The way I was treated in Morocco made me feel at home. Not that I've ever done otherwise but it reminded me to always treat strangers with kindness.

I paid for the extra day we spent in the Sahara and left a

more than generous tip. I didn't tell Khalid for fear he would give it back. He took the money without counting. Then he asked if I had enough cash to pay for a taxi in Casablanca to the airport. He said if not, I could keep the cash and pay online when I arrived at my next stop, Cameroon. I couldn't believe his kindness.

When it was time, we went back to the train station. The train was almost 20 minutes late. I boarded and, as usual, the men wouldn't let me lift my suitcase. My fellow passenger on the train, the older gentleman who helped put away my suitcase, had more recommendations for me. Chawel, or at least that's what it sounded like, is a small town in the north of Morocco where you can go hiking in the mountains away from most touristy areas. He told me of another small town near Fes where one can visit hot springs. Regarding the desert, he said the desert is different at different seasons. The best time, in his opinion, is spring or autumn. I plan to return to Morocco first chance I get and I will be sure to visit these places, *Inshallah*.

I'd gotten tons of compliments on my braids everywhere I'd been, from Argentina to Morocco. The old guy sitting next to me on the train to Casablanca commented on my "belle cheveux" or pretty hair. It was ironic because I was getting tired of it. I was also tired of being covered up. That day, I was wearing a t-shirt, a thermal top, a fleece, a sweater over it, a scarf, and a jacket. I hadn't seen my neck in weeks. I couldn't wait to be warm and free again. I missed my own body.

I had more adventures going through immigration in Casablanca. My bags were too heavy but the officials eventually let me pass without paying extra. Mind you, I was willing to return to the counter and check my suitcase. They even helped me fill out my immigration forms. I boarded the plane a very sad person because I didn't want to leave this beautiful country full of the most beautiful people you'll ever meet, inside and out. I can't wait to come back, *Inshallah*.

Tips for travel to Morocco

- Allow for enough days, at least 4, if you would like to visit the Sahara Desert.

- If visiting in the winter, pack warm clothes.

- Take a covering for your nose and mouth if you go to the desert.

- Pack your camera in a plastic bag to prevent damage from sand in the desert.

- Don't take unnecessary risks like going off with strangers.

Cameroon

Independence Monument

My flight arrived in Douala, Cameroon at 3 am. I stood outside for five minutes looking for my brother and sister who were supposed to pick me up. When I didn't see them, I had the horrible thought that there had been some miscommunication on dates of travel and they had not shown up. My gears started grinding as I thought of alternate plans. I heaved a huge sigh of relief when my brother Eric suddenly popped up in front of me. My sister Shannon soon followed.

After all the hugs, the inevitable question came up,

"Where's Fluffy?"

My sister had been following me on Instagram and apparently had fallen in love with Fluffums. After she got properly acquainted with Fluffy, we got into the car and headed for the town of Buea.

I shared pictures and stories of my travels, and they updated me on things happening in Cameroon. An hour and a half later, we made it home. I went straight to sleep.

Beetles prepared for scientific research

When I woke up, it was late morning. My sister fussed over me, spoiling me and cooking for me. It felt good to be home. She left to go handle school stuff but my brother and I hung around all afternoon, playing chess while waiting for my dad. The neighbor had a business where he caught and preserved insects for sale, primarily for research purposes. We marveled at some of his beetles while we waited.

My dad lived in the next town but came to Buea every week to lecture at the University of Buea. My dad having a PhD was obviously a huge factor in me getting a doctorate. It was just expected that I would follow in his footsteps. I was so happy to see him when he finally showed up. We are all growing older but he was managing to do it gracefully. Still, I hated that he sounded older, even in person. After a couple hours, he left to go back to his place in the next town. He maintains two households, one for himself in the next town since his primary university lecturing job is based there, and one for my siblings, two of whom were finishing medical school. Apparently we had a cat, Misty, but my dad hated that it would sit on his favorite chair and leave hair on it, so we had to keep Misty outside every time he was around.

I had paid for most of my sisters' medical school tuition and expenses. I was really proud that Kathy had graduated and Shannon was working on her thesis and was six months away from graduating herself. Once she was done, I would be focusing a lot more on myself.

After my dad left, Eric and I went to the soon-to-be-opened mall and he showed me around. He was helping the owners with security systems and online marketing so he had free rein. Afterwards, we went to grab smoothies, then dinner.

The next day, Shannon decided I had to change my hair. Bossiness runs in my family. The thing is, I was really tired of my hairstyle so I let it happen. The salon we went to served us champagne while they did my hair, but the actual workmanship was shoddy at best. I had to live with it though and make the best of it. I only had 4 days in Cameroon, and I wasn't going to waste another whole day on hair alone.

My other sister Kathy came to visit that evening. She had just started a new job in the next town so she was living with my dad there. Apparently, he was already asking her when she would be moving out. We had a good laugh at that. The hospital she was working for had provided her a house but it was not yet ready for her to move into. My poor dad was stuck with her for a few more weeks. He is a loner, and I could only imagine his chagrin at finally having a house to himself, only to have one of us move back in with him.

The next morning, I woke up to the pleasant sound of Kathy singing as she moved about. She really has a beautiful voice. My nieces Tina and Lucy came to visit and spent all day with us. To describe 10 year old Tina as precocious would be an understatement. The child has no fear of anyone or anything. This will serve her well in life but makes for quite a few minor heart attacks when she is in one's care. I learned that she had even talked her way into a music video for a well-known Cameroonian artist. It probably didn't hurt that my brother was involved with making and editing music videos for top Cameroonian artists. The one thing Tina is afraid of is Misty the cat. They are equally terrified of each other. The dance they do when one must pass near the other is hilarious to watch.

Cameroon is a very green country, especially the southern parts which are equatorial. At that time, early December, it was cool in the mornings in Buea, around 60°F, but would quickly warm up. Buea is at the foot of Mt. Cameroon, which stands at 13,255 feet. The mountain is an active volcano which had its last sustained eruption in 2000, although there was a brief eruption in 2012. The volcanic activity makes the area very fertile. Thus, food is cheap and very plentiful in the country. Every year in February, the Mount Cameroon race is run by both locals and foreigners alike. Unfortunately, the mountain was shrouded in clouds and mist during my entire stay so I couldn't get a clear view or picture of it.

Beautiful greenery of Cameroon

Cameroon has both English and French as its official languages, though French is much more widely spoken. There are over 200 distinct languages spoken in Cameroon. Pidgin English is also spoken in the English-speaking parts of the country.

Getting around is easy as there are numerous cabs driving by from dawn till late at night. Just be prepared to share the cab with other passengers. It's worth it because it keeps the fares low. Most rides cost less than a dollar to anywhere in Buea. Motorcycles are also prevalent although considered dangerous because helmets are not mandatory by law. The main roads in Buea are good although side roads are often unpaved.

Cameroon is in the malaria zone. Malaria is like the African equivalent of the flu. The flu is actually not as common in Africa as it is in the US. I've had malaria twice, and my clearest memory of it is aching joints and fever. I started taking my anti-malaria medication a few days before leaving Morocco. I took one pill a day while I was in the malaria zone and continued for a week after.

Most transactions in Cameroon are done with cash. Bargaining or haggling over prices is the norm. It can get tiring to haggle over everything; I usually let my siblings handle it for me. Once you get to know Cameroonians, they are extremely generous and hospitable.

Like with most francophone countries, it is advisable to carry identification at all times. Checkpoints are common when traveling between cities and lack of identification can land you in trouble.

We took my nieces to see the monument celebrating fifty years of Cameroonian independence. Then we caught a bus to the nearby town of Limbé to see family friends. Tina had spent a couple months with them the previous summer. As we walked towards the house, word was spreading that Tina was in town. By the time we got there, there was a sizable crowd of children and adults waiting to see her. The mother of the house arrived from work an hour later, and said she had been given word that Tina was around long before she got to the house. I was lost for words that a 10 year old could wield such influence. I only hoped in the future, she would use her charisma for good.

The following day, Eric, Shannon and I went to see Kathy and my dad. We went to see my dad first at his house. I explained that I was taking a trip around the world. The look on his face was priceless but would have been terrifying when I was a child. This is why I hadn't told him about the trip when I first saw him in Buea. He seemed lost for words. After thinking it over, he said he thought it was a good idea. It would enable me to clear my head before taking the next steps. I showed him pictures of my trip and was rewarded with sounds of wonder. Of the picture of Antarctica, he said,

"You've really been there? That's fantastic."

I was surprised that he was surprised because I get my love of travel from him. I loved that he worked and studied all over the world. Maybe the difference was that I was only doing it for pleasure.

My siblings, myself and Fluffums in Kathy's office

The visit came to an end and I bade my dad farewell until my next visit to Cameroon. He made me promise to be careful on my travels. He also gave me a list of people in Buea he thought I should see before I left. It was a long list. I persuaded him to take a picture with Fluffy, then we left for Kathy's office.

Dr. Kathy was wrapping up when we got there. I still had a cough from being in the Sahara Desert. Kathy and Shannon consulted with each other then Kathy wrote out a prescription for some medicine for me. That is, to date, the proudest moment of my life. We had dinner, then she put us on a bus back to Buea.

The next day was my last in Cameroon. Eric had to travel for work so it was just Shannon and me. I looked at the list from my dad and decided to prioritize. The top of the list were family friends whom we have known all our lives. I always make time to see them when I am in Cameroon. We showed up at their house without warning. This is how things are done over there. It wouldn't have mattered if only one person was home. The fact that we showed up would have still meant a lot. We were fed as is the norm, and we ate obediently.

For the sake of politeness, we stayed for several hours. When we finally left, it felt like the sun was at its most intense. Shannon and I looked at each other, looked at the list, and decided

"F*@# this sh*t."

We just couldn't do it. We were tired from the sun and sleepy from all the food we had eaten. We went home and took a long nap. Going home is work because it's considered impolite not to check in with everyone you know. I did nothing touristic because I knew there wouldn't be enough time.

We woke up in the evening and went out for suya, or grilled savory kebabs. As I munched on them, I made peace with the fact that this was my last night in Cameroon and my last night with my family. It was probably just as well since Shannon had not worked on her thesis the whole time I'd been there.

I left all my warm clothes behind: my winter jackets, my sweater, and those heavy boots. I kept a fleece just in case I ended up somewhere unexpectedly chilly.

We arranged for a car and driver to take us to the airport. We left before dawn so we could have enough time to deal with traffic in Douala. In the car, I heard a song I'd never heard before which I just had to have. I Shazamed it and when I got to Wi-Fi, I saw that it was "Papilo" by Beverly. It was a love song with a really cool beat sung in Pidgin English by a woman about how her lover is her hero. When we got to the airport, I checked in, then Shannon and I had breakfast. Eventually, we reluctantly parted and I went through security. My next destination was Kigali, Rwanda.

Tips for travel to Cameroon

- Get Yellow Fever vaccine and certificate. You will need them to enter Cameroon.

- Take anti-malarial medication.

- Credit cards are rarely accepted. Carry cash or get cash from ATMs.

- Keep enough cash in Franc CFA to pay airport tax when you fly out of the country.

- Learn how to haggle.

Rwanda

Sunrise outside Kigali

I was heading to Rwanda, *le pays des milles collines*, the land of a thousand hills. The flight from Douala had a technical stop in Brazzaville. This time I was awake and knew to stay on the plane. My seatmates were Nigerian businessmen living in Congo Brazzaville. They would travel back and forth to Cameroon and Nigeria to buy things to sell in the Congo. I was not surprised when they told me they were part of a large Nigerian community in the country. Nigerians seem to thrive everywhere. We exchanged contact information and they disembarked.

I finally arrived in Kigali late in the afternoon. I had to buy a visa at the airport and I was gratified to see that I could use my credit card rather than the limited cash I had. Later still, I found out that some ATMs in Rwanda dispense US Dollars and I made sure to get enough before I left the country. The most widely spoken languages in Rwanda are French, English and

Kinyarwanda.

I caught a cab to my hotel. It was raining lightly. Temperatures were cool, in the high 60s. I hoped I wouldn't regret leaving my jackets behind. My hotel was in the center of town and it was rush hour so there was a lot of traffic to deal with. Just like Morocco and Cameroon, there were a lot of motorcycle taxis but in Rwanda, both the driver and passenger have to wear helmets by law. I later learned there is a 10,000 Franc fine paid by the driver if either himself or his passenger is not wearing a helmet. Not wearing a seatbelt, and driving while talking on the phone are also against the law. Once a month, there is a mandatory cleaning day for all Rwandans. Rwanda reminded me very much of Cameroon with its green vegetation and tropical weather, except it was much more orderly.

The streets of Kigali

I checked into the hotel and was very pleased with my room. From my balcony, I could enjoy the sights and sounds of the city. There was a mosquito net over my bed. That night, I was tormented by mosquitoes every time I stepped outside the net. I finally discovered that the maids had left all the windows open. The mosquitoes were pouring in like they were having a party.

My first impression of Kigali was that it is very clean and orderly. The one unnerving thing was that on a lot of street corners, there were police and soldiers standing with weapons. I watched how people behaved around them and for the most part people went about their business ignoring them. Occasionally, someone would engage a soldier and they always responded although they remained focused on their task. I found out that soldiers on the street corners have been the norm since the end of the genocide. It was meant to instill a sense of safety. The posts are manned 24/7 in five hour shifts.

I could see why Rwanda is called the "land of a thousand hills. There were innumerable rolling hills around Kigali. At night, I could see the lights on the hills from my hotel room.

I slept in the next morning, trying to regain my strength. Traveling can be tiring. I had a gorilla trek booked for the following day. I kept this day open in case I didn't feel like doing anything. The hotel had a decent restaurant so I decided to have lunch there. At one point, a flying critter fell into my mango juice. The waiter was very courteous and had some fresh juice made. When he brought it to me he said,

"God will protect."

meaning,

"You'll probably be okay even if something else falls in and you drink it."

I had a good laugh at that. After lunch, I got itchy feet. I went for a walk, taking my passport and credit cards with me, to be prepared for any opportunity. I found some art shops and I had to fight myself to not buy anything since the space in my luggage was extremely limited.

I continued my walk and by chance found a travel agency. I decided why not, and walked in. I booked a tour of Kigali with them, and they sent me off with a car and driver. John, my driver, gave me a thorough tour of Kigali. The most memorable part was the Kigali Genocide Museum where I spent a few hours.

The genocide happened in 1994 but the story really begins with colonization by the Belgians, which began in 1923 and continued until independence in 1962. Rwandans were originally split into about 18 different clans. Within the clans, there were 3 socioeconomic classifications which could change if personal circumstances changed: Hutu, Tutsi and Twa. The Belgians made these classifications racial in 1932, forcing anyone with more than 10 cows to be Tutsi, anyone with less than 10 cows to be Hutu, and this would apply to their descendants. This forced divide began to create tension. The Belgians treated the Tutsis like they were more intelligent, and gave some of them the opportunity to get some education. They claimed the Tutsis were an alien race, and used physical features to differentiate between the Tutsis and the "indigenous" Hutus. In the 1930s, the Belgians forced Rwandans to carry identity cards, counting 15% as Tutsi, 84% as Hutu, and 1% as Twa. The

Twa people are pygmies and are thus ethnically distinct.

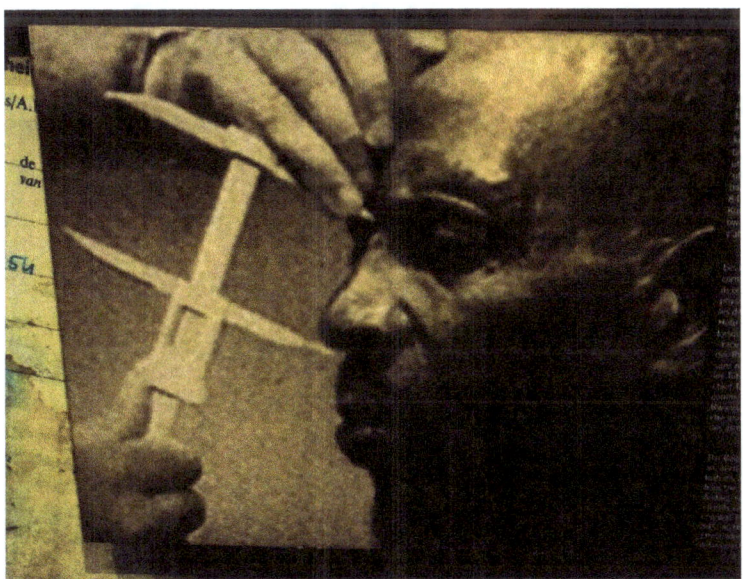

A Belgian measuring a Rwandan's face to determine whether he should be Hutu or Tutsi

In 1959, the Belgian Bishop Perraudin portrayed the majority Hutus as being oppressed by the Tutsis. This tension resulted in violence over the years, culminating in the genocide in 1994. Even then, other nations had a hand. France armed and trained the Hutu militia, then provided a safe zone for them and an escape route into the Democratic Republic of Congo.

It's well known that the UN made no effort to intervene even though it had troops on the ground. Instead those troops were told not to intervene, and were finally withdrawn. The world did nothing as millions were slaughtered.

French troops collected Tutsi survivors from the hills, assuring them it was now safe then left. The survivors emerged only to be attacked and killed by the Interahamwe, the Hutu militia.

Paul Kagame, the current President, was in Uganda during this time, working as part of Yoweri Museveni's government. He and others assembled a group, the Rwandan Patriotic Front, the RPF, and they fought their way to Kigali, disarming the Hutu militia as they went. It was during this time that France provided safe haven for the militia who were the perpetrators of the genocide.

After quelling the genocide, the RPF formed a new government and provided security. It encouraged Rwandans to rebuild their lives without taking revenge, which is admirable and difficult for me to imagine. The government set up Gacaca, meaning grass, courts which brought everyone together including victims, perpetrators and witnesses, in front of judges. The aim was to establish the truth of what happened, and determine punishment for the perpetrators. Those confessing could choose to serve half of their sentence in community service, e.g. building roads and homes for survivors. Those who didn't had to serve their full sentence in prison.

Over 10 years, almost 2 million cases were tried in over 12,000 Gacaca courts. Gacaca has been the most comprehensive post-conflict justice system to date, providing justice and the opportunity for truth-telling. Gacaca fostered restitution between survivors and perpetrators while providing an environment of deterrence. Thus, it played a big part in providing peace and reconciliation.

I knew the story well, but it was difficult to maintain my composure in the museum, reading how friends and neighbors had turned on each other. The betrayal by priests and nuns was even more sickening. On the other hand, the courage of those who had sheltered and hidden others should be applauded. Many of them have gone unsung but I was glad to read the names and stories of many of them in the museum.

I moved on to the section devoted to children who died during the genocide. A quote outside the room said,

"Not even the innocent survived."

I tried to read about these children, their hopes and dreams, their last words, and how they died. Five minutes and I could take no more. It was just too sad.

The last part of the museum was dedicated to genocides that had taken place in other parts of the world. The Holocaust in Germany, the Khmer Rouge in Cambodia against the Vietnamese, the German genocide of the Herero and Namaqua in Namibia, etc. A common theme was that genocide was never spontaneous. People don't just wake up one day and start killing their neighbors. It starts with identification of a particular group as the source of all of a nation's problems, followed by hate speech against that group. This can go on for years, increasing in intensity which eventually leads to violence. This is why we must not condone hate speech of any kind against anyone. That is why comments made by people like Donald Trump are especially concerning. If you are thinking you don't want to be involved, remember, today me, tomorrow you. Reverend Niemoeller, a Protestant priest who was put in a concentration camp by the Nazis for seven years, put it eloquently:

"First they came for the Communists,
and I did not speak up-
because I was not a Communist.
Then they came for the Jews,
and I did not speak up-

because I was not a Jew.
Then they came for the Trade Unionists,
and I did not speak up-
because I was not a Trade Unionist.
Then they came for the Catholics,
and I did not speak up-
because I was a Protestant.
Then they came for me-
and by that time,
Nobody was left to speak up."

At the museum, I met soccer players from Kenya who were in town for some games. I also met businessmen from South Sudan in town for a logistics convention. I was glad to meet them but the history around us was so sobering. I was still lost for words when I left.

My driver John told me that they are encouraged to speak openly about the genocide. Still, I could not bring myself to ask him which side he had been on in 1994. Considering everything I had learned, I was doubly impressed with the current state of Rwanda. The fact that people could live together in peace today, forgiving each other and moving on with life, is not trivial. It is nothing short of a miracle.

By this point, I was starting to realize that Rwandans didn't smile much. Everyone I came into contact with was competent and treated me well, but without a smile. If you can get past that, you will enjoy the country. After visiting the Kigali Genocide Museum, I reasoned that country's history might have something to do with the service without a smile. One of the clips showed a woman saying her neighbors, whom her family used to do everything with, actually killed her family. She said she has had a hard time trusting anyone after that. That certainly explains why they don't smile until after they get to know you, and don't open up much even then. I had a hard time connecting with Rwandans. They weren't rude or unfriendly. Just kind of aloof.

The driving tour of Kigali continued. We drove through Nyarutarama, the residential area for rich people; Nyabugogo, the bustling bus park with buses going all around the country and to nearby countries as well; the predominantly Moslem part; and the Milles Collines Hotel which the movie Hotel Rwanda is based on.

It was late at night when the tour finally ended. I thanked John and he dropped me off at my hotel. Dinner was a quiet affair as I continued musing on the things I had read at the museum. I had to be up very early so I was in bed by 9 pm. This time I made sure the windows were closed before I turned in.

My guide, Jack, picked me up on time at 4:30 am. Jack lived in neighboring Uganda but often drove into Rwanda to give tours. As usual I rode in the front because it makes for better photos, and it's easier to ask the guide questions. It was about 70°F outside but the temperature kept dropping as we drove further outside the city and as the rain picked up. It fell below 60°F on the two hour drive to Volcano National Park, where we would find the gorillas. Gorilla trekking was something I had dreamed of since 2004 when one of my mentors showed me pictures of her trip to Uganda. I couldn't believe yet another bucket list item was finally coming true.

The gorillas can be seen either from Uganda or Rwanda. I

chose Rwanda because I have always wanted to visit Rwanda for myself. Coincidentally, it takes less time to get to the gorillas in Rwanda than in Uganda. Another benefit is that one gets to see the Virunga Mountains as well.

As we drove, we saw women walking with firewood on their heads to sell to restaurants in town. The road was windy through the mountains which were lush with trees and vegetation. The sunrise was spectacular with the mist on the mountains and the golden sun rising on the horizon and kissing the clouds.

When we arrived at the park, I joined several other tourists and we watched cultural dances which were reminiscent of South African dances especially the jumping. Next, we were given a briefing on how to behave around the gorillas. For instance, we were told that if the gorillas charged us, especially the silverback leader, we were to stand still and not make eye contact. Then we were supposed to kneel in front of him and make a guttural sound to appease him. Running away would suggest that we came with ill intentions, and we would surely be chased and beaten to death. Kneeling is non-threatening and shows subservience. I sincerely hoped I would remember everything we were being told.

The family of gorillas my group would be following was the Agashya, meaning something special. The group consisted of the silverback father, his wives and their children ranging from babies to adult gorillas. At the time, Agashya had about 23 members.

The trek into the forests on the Virunga Mountains started with a slight drizzle then thankfully the sun came out. It generally takes about three hours of trekking to find the gorillas, which means a total of six hours trekking for the day. We were lucky because they were nearby and we were able to see them after only an hour. We spent a solid hour with the Agashya, watching the babies frolic on their parent's backs, and the young males pulling down eucalyptus leaves as they showed off to us. The guides were wonderful. It was obvious they knew the gorillas really well. They were very familiar with the mannerisms of the whole family and knew how to prepare for whatever was coming next.

Silverback gorilla and his baby

At one point, the silverback charged at me. I don't know why but I suspect it had to do with one of the American tourists. She kept stepping too close to the gorillas, and ignoring what the guides were telling us. At one point, one of the guides had to physically pull her back as she was too close to the silverback. I think the gorilla became agitated because of this. It's possible he was charging all of us and not just me, but I can't be sure as it happened so quickly.

I had paid attention during the briefing but my reaction was instinctive. I immediately turned to run. Luckily, one of the guides had been paying attention to the silverback's body language. He was standing right behind me so that there was no room for me to turn. He grabbed my shoulder and said very calmly,

"Relax."

I came to my senses, and by then the silverback had returned to his children. The whole incident was over in ten seconds. If the silverback had wanted to do damage, there's not much we could have done to stop him. That was a sobering reminder to always respect nature.

After an hour, the guides said it was time to go. As we left the forest, the gorillas followed us, posing and showing off the whole way. As we descended into the valley, they stayed on the mountain watching us. I learned that the gorilla population has been increasing due to efforts against poaching. In fact, the last recorded poaching incident was in 2002. We were given certificates showing that we had participated in the gorilla trek.

I had been wearing jeans almost every day for a month and a half and I was tired of them. I broke my no shopping rule and bought loose-fitting and very colorful pants. They would take up minimal space and allow my legs to breathe when I wore them, if I absolutely had to wear pants.

My shoes and jeans were covered in mud from slipping and sliding through the wet forest. I felt bad about muddying up the inside of the SUV but Jack said he had seen much worse. We had lunch before heading back to Kigali. At lunch, we met a young man who was planning a trip from Cape Town to Cairo the following year. We had a great chat about traveling in general. I decided that Cape Town to Cairo could be my next adventure.

On the drive back to Kigali, I admired the crops on the mountains around us. Rwanda is very fertile. The volcanic soil around the Virunga Mountains makes agriculture easy. Crops grown in the country include rice, wheat, peas, potatoes, corn, bananas, sugarcane, cassava, coffee, and tea.

Jack asked what my plans were for the rest of my stay. I had two days left in Rwanda but no plans and I told him as much. He asked if I was interested in going to Lake Bunyonyi in Uganda for a day. Many thoughts went through my head. Although Uganda was not in my original itinerary, I was tired of not getting smiles from people I interacted with in Rwanda. I decided

"F*@# this sh*t."

I had no hotel reservations to cancel so I agreed.

On the way back to Kigali, we were pulled over for passing a car too close to a bend. Jack's license was taken away and he was given a ticket. He would only get the license back after paying the ticket. Then he would have to return to where he was given the ticket to show them the receipt and pick up his license. There was no getting out of this ticket. In Rwanda, rules are rules. I found out later that after he dropped me off, Jack paid off the ticket and returned to get his license.

That night I had dinner at my hotel with an old friend from high school. She and her husband and I spent several hours together then parted ways. I cleaned the mud off my shoes and my jeans and went to bed, exhausted. The next morning, Jack picked me up bright and early and we

drove to the border. It was raining again.

Jack was not much of a talker. To add to that, he only had one CD in the car, the same one we had listened to the day before. I got so sick of Avril Lavigne. Eventually, I asked him to turn the CD player off and we drove in silence. I started to develop an even greater appreciation for Khalid, my guide in Morocco. Jack never volunteered information, although he responded if he was asked a question.

We arrived at the border and exited Rwanda. We went to the Uganda side and I bought a visa. It was more expensive than I'd expected. I recommend buying the East African Tourist Visa which gets you into Uganda, Rwanda and Kenya. This was my very first land border crossing and it made me appreciate flying. It was quick but not easy to know which building to go to next. I was glad Jack was there to show me the way.

Jack said Rwanda had too many rules compared to Uganda. It made me wonder what Uganda would be like.

Tips for travel to Rwanda

- Book gorilla trek in advance as permits need to be purchased in advance.

- Listen to your guides when dealing with wildlife.

- For the gorilla trek, wear clothes and shoes you don't mind getting mud on.

- Get a multiple entry visa or an East African Tourist Visa if you intend to travel to Uganda, Kenya or Rwanda.

- Don't ask people about what they went through or did during the genocide. That's just rude.

- Credit cards are accepted in a lot of places. If you need cash, some ATMs dispense both Rwandan Francs and US dollars.

- Credit cards are accepted at the airport for visa purchase for eligible countries.

Uganda

Lake Bunyonyi

In Rwanda, cars drive on the right. As soon as we crossed the border, we had to switch to the left because in Uganda, cars drive on the left. Uganda is also one hour ahead of Rwanda. I noticed motorcycle taxis were present in Uganda, but helmets were optional.

The rolling, green, vegetation-covered hills continue from Rwanda to Uganda. The hills are covered by crops grown on terraces. Crops and houses can be seen perched precariously on the steep slopes.

Jack visibly relaxed and even became more talkative. He expressed that in his opinion, Uganda was much better than Rwanda. I asked in what way. He said Rwanda has too many rules. He gave an example of a small car accident. If it occurred in Rwanda, the police have to be called, no matter how slight the accident. In Uganda, the affected parties can work things out without involving the police. Other people seemed to corroborate these sentiments. I was told by more than one person,

> "In Uganda, you can buy a plot of land. From sunup to sundown, no one will ask you any questions about it."

I assume that means you would get questions in Rwanda.

We drove to the tiny town of Kabale which is on the shores of Lake Bunyonyi. Bunyonyi means "little birds" as many birds live around the lake. The lake is surrounded by green hills covered in trees and crops. It is said to be around 2,900 feet at its deepest point, which would make it the second largest lake in Africa. It has about twenty nine islands. Punishment Island was where girls pregnant out of wedlock were dropped off in disgrace. If they were lucky, they were rescued by passersby.

In town, we first met up with Jack's sister, Ruth. She was very bubbly and much more talkative and informative than her brother. I took to her instantly. She worked for a European NGO that provided Pygmy children with an education. She seemed really passionate about her job.

We left her and picked up another guide, Robert. Thankfully, Robert was a much better communicator than Jack. We found a hotel that had vacancies. It was beautifully designed and right on the shores of the lake. I dropped my stuff off in my room and we headed out to go visit the Batwa, or Twa, Pygmies. As they are pygmies, they are of diminutive stature.

We spent a few hours with the Batwa. Climbing the hills to get to their village was hard work. One of the Batwa let us into his house. He was newly married and lived there with his wife. The house was made of clay and grass. The inside was a single room which functioned as both bedroom and kitchen. At the time, there was food cooking inside so the house was very smoky. There was a bed made from wood and grass and lifted off the ground. A pile of potatoes were stored in the corner. Our host's wife was away working on their farm so we didn't get to meet her. This represents quite a change in the times as traditionally, the Batwa were hunters. I remember learning about the Pygmies when I was in primary school. Meeting them was yet another dream come true for me. Being flexible in my schedule had allowed this to happen for me.

Fluffikins and myself with a Batwa Pygmy

As we drove back to town, Robert asked me to set up a GoFundMe for the Batwa Pygmies to raise money for them. He felt like they are very poor so they need to be helped. I told him that could easily be done but it would not be done by me. Unfortunately I never got a chance to explain that I'm not a heartless person. I know that simply giving anyone money is not going to help them. It makes more sense to help them generate money by teaching them useful, marketable skills. Teaching them to fish rather than giving them fish, if you will. Charity creates an unequal relationship, putting the giver above the receiver. Having visited the Batwa for myself, I saw nothing wrong with the way they were living. It's how they've always lived and they were content. It seemed pretentious for anyone to drag them to a different way of living, especially by the unsustainable means of giving them money they hadn't earned. If the money dried up for any reason, they would be worse off.

Before my guides dropped me off at my hotel, we stopped to see Ruth. Her organization was having a Christmas party for the Pygmy children. It was a fun event with lots of music and dancing. Other organizations had pitched in to provide toys and candy for the kids who appeared to range in age from 5 to 14.

I have thought a lot about the wisdom of taking children that young away from their parents. The idea is to provide them with education that allows them to compete with the rest of the world. It sounded great in theory but something about it bothered me. The children live in a boarding house and are away from their parents except for a few days every year. I remember reading articles about similar practices carried out on Native Americans in the US and First Nations in Canada. Those who went through this give testimony of the psychological damage done to them by this barbaric practice. There has to be a compromise; perhaps a school close to where the Batwa live so they can have a modern education but still learn their own cultures and live with their parents.

It was very late when we got back to my hotel. All the guests had turned in for the night but the staff were kind enough to make me a very late dinner, which was delicious. I took a shower and fell fast asleep.

In the morning, I was awoken by the songs of what sounded like a thousand birds. Lake Bunyonyi must be heaven for bird watchers. I stepped on the balcony and admired the beauty of the lake and the hills and flowers around it. The smell of smoke in my hair reminded me of my visit with the Pygmies. I smiled a very satisfied smile.

View of Lake Bunyonyi from my room balcony

The agenda for the day was to go for a boat ride on the

lake then return to Rwanda so I could catch a plane to my next destination, Zambia. After breakfast, I took time to explore the amazing hotel I was staying in. There was a pool, a pool table and various other amenities. More than anything, the beauty of the place held me and I didn't want to leave.

Eventually, I did leave so we could tour the lake. The day was cool and hazy. On the boat, I lost a zipper from the boots I bought in Argentina. I had had to replace the zipper in Cameroon and I was fed up with the boots. I vowed to replace them as soon as I could. We cruised around the lake then headed for Bushara Island and spent some time walking around and exploring it. There are lodges and campsites on the island, as well as a restaurant and gift shop. Afterwards, we headed back to the hotel and I checked out.

Paddler on Lake Bunyonyi

We stopped at a restaurant in Kabale for lunch. We had a buffet meal of sweet beef, mashed bananas, goat meat soup, sweet potatoes, rice and beans. The sweet beef and sweet potatoes were my favorite.

After lunch, we headed to the border and we got out to show our documents to the immigration officials. Robert's wallet was not in his pocket and we couldn't find it anywhere. We searched for almost 20 minutes. As Robert stood there looking miserable, a man came up to us and gave him the wallet. He had apparently picked it up on the ground. Everything was intact in the wallet and I marveled at the man's honesty and kindness.

Getting through the Uganda side was fast and easy. On the Rwandan side, it took almost half an hour for what I assume was some kind of background check on myself to be completed. I then had to go to a nearby bank to pay for the visa before returning with the receipt. After I presented the receipt, my passport was finally stamped. We got back in the SUV and headed for Kigali International Airport.

We were still playing the same damn CD from the last couple of days. I didn't really like my guide Jack. After three days with him, sometimes I looked at him and almost hated him. Again, I appreciated how awesome Khalid had been. The second guide Robert was much better but they tended to talk to each other a lot in Swahili, which I don't understand.

I just wanted to get to the airport so I could be done with them. I thought,

"F*@# this sh*t."

I put in my earphones and blasted music that was not Avril Lavigne, and closed my eyes.

Flying out from Kigali was uneventful. I had to check my suitcase but that gave me more freedom to walk through the gift shops. I found a suitable refrigerator magnet then waited for my flight to be called. In Zambia, I would be staying with an old classmate from high school. I WhatsApp'ed her to make sure she would be picking me up. I also WhatsApp'ed my dear friend Kibs telling her how my trip was going. As usual, she didn't respond even though I could tell she was reading my messages. In fact, I hadn't heard back from her since I told her about Antarctica. I figured she must be really busy. Then I sat back and waited for my flight to be called.

Tips for travel to Uganda

- Get the East African Tourist Visa to give you flexibility to also visit Rwanda and Kenya.

- In the rainy season (October to December, March to May), the ground gets very muddy. Wear closed shoes.

- Take cash. Credit cards are not accepted everywhere. You can get cash at ATMs using your debit card.

- If going gorilla trekking, schedule a day or two afterwards to recuperate.

Zambia

Impala

It was after 9 pm when my flight arrived in Lusaka, Zambia. I went through immigration with no problem. The visa took up a whole page in my passport and I realized I only had 2 free pages left. I needed to figure out a solution as I was only halfway through my trip. After picking up my bag, I scanned the crowd and saw my dear friend Susie. Her son and daughter ran to me and hugged me before she could. Apparently they'd been following my trip on social media so they recognized me immediately.

Susie and I had been great friends in high school. I hadn't been back to the country in a long time but we had kept in touch through all the years. She looked exactly the same as the last time I saw her. We hugged it out, hardly believing we were meeting again after so many years.

As we drove to her house, she filled me in on her life. The biggest shocker was that she was going through a divorce. We had been in constant touch for the last few months so I was really surprised she hadn't mentioned it before. The kids were in the car so I didn't press her for details. But I became determined to keep in better touch with people I care about.

We got to the house, and I met her live-in cook and nanny. They had dinner ready for me and I ate gladly. Susie and I stayed up talking for a while after everyone else went to bed. It was 2 o'clock in the morning before we finally turned in.

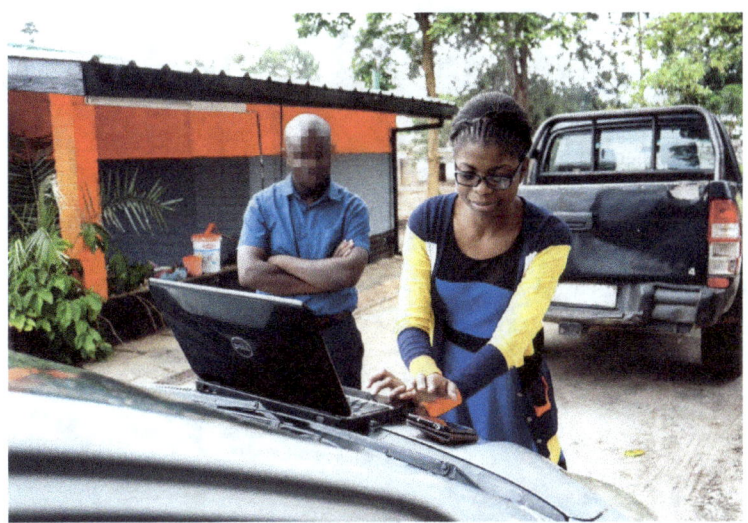

Susie meeting with a client at his work site

I slept in the following day. When I finally woke up and got ready, we headed out to Manda Hill Mall, which is the oldest mall in Lusaka. I was still hoping for a decent pair of boots after the zipper popped off my current pair. I didn't find any I loved but I did buy a dress so I could feel like a woman again.

We had dinner at a Chinese restaurant at the mall. The food was really good so we got some to go for the kids.

Nothing good was playing at the movies so we headed back to the house. We fought the rush hour traffic and finally made it home. I noted that unlike the other African countries I had visited on this trip, Zambia did not have any motorcycle taxis.

Outside Manda Hill Mall in Lusaka

I only had four days in Zambia and I had no solid plans beyond wanting to visit Victoria Falls. Visiting our old high school was another option but it was close to Christmas and so schools were on break. If we visited, we wouldn't even be able to see our old teachers.

Susie is a freelance architect so she sets her own schedule. The kids were on break but fortunately, the nanny and the cook took care of them when Susie was busy. She was able to share in all my adventures because she worked for herself. When she had deadlines pending, she would go to bed early, then wake up at 2 am and work until about 6 am. Then she would sleep for a couple hours and we would leave for the day. It showed me yet another way to live that I had never considered for myself. I love to travel and if I worked for myself, I could travel whenever I wanted. I was really inspired and I kept that in the back of my mind.

Susie's sister suggested we visit a game reserve that is close to Lusaka. Besides game drives, there were plenty of other activities to do. We decided to make a whole day of it and headed there early one morning.

Resting lions

The resort was picturesque with beautiful Zambian art displayed all over the facilities. There were several activities we could do but we decided on a game drive first. The guide was very knowledgeable about the animals which made the drive very interesting. We saw lynxes, cheetahs, lions, zebra, giraffes, impala, and elephants, to name a few. After the game drive, we went for a boat ride on a manmade lake on the grounds. The other ladies in the boat were hilarious, screaming at the tops of their lungs but still enjoying themselves. We all had a good time.

Kissing a cheetah

Lunch was next and it was buffet-style. The most exotic part of the meal was Chikanda, also called African polony, which looks and tastes like regular polony. However, it is non-meat and is made from orchid tubers. It had been years since I'd had it so I was glad the staff had made the effort.

Our next activity was walking cheetahs. There was a pair of cheetahs which had been brought up at the reserve, and had been trained to be walked from the time they were cubs. Still, I listened carefully as were given instructions on how to behave around them. The encounter with the gorillas was still fresh on my mind. We were encouraged to pet the cheetahs everywhere except for their tummies. Their tummies were ticklish and they might try to also "play" with us. We petted them then walked them holding their tails. Anyone who has played with a cat knows that cats hate it when their tails are touched. So I was skeptical when we were encouraged to pet the cheetahs' tails. They actually seemed to love it. We walked single file behind the cheetahs, holding their leashes but allowing them to lead so they could see where they were going. Being so close to them was mind-blowing. Susie was completely comfortable with them even laying her head on their backs.

The next activity was horse-back riding. It was Susie's first time so the ride was short, only about 30 minutes. She enjoyed it immensely and vowed to bring her kids there as soon as she could. We decided to make this our last activity. We ended the day by taking a dip in the pool. All in all, it was a wonderful day. I was glad to see my friend enjoy herself so much. She didn't appear to carry her problems with her but I was still glad to provide a distraction.

I was having such a good time that I ended up extending my stay by a few days. My next stop was supposed to be South Africa but I decided to go to Zimbabwe first. I got in touch with my travel agents and had them make the changes. I sent Kibs my new arrival date in Cape Town and she wished me well in Zambia and Zimbabwe.

Because Susie is an architect, I got to see Lusaka through an architect's eyes. There was a lot of building going on, and a lot of plots being bought and sold. The city was expanding and areas that were previously well on the outskirts were now firmly a part of the city of Lusaka. Plots were even being bought in areas that had little road access. Eventually, better roads would be built to these areas making them more accessible. As soon as that happened, prices would shoot up. Susie seemed to have her hand on the pulse of the city and knew the best places to buy before prices went up.

It was mango season and they were abundant and plentiful. We bought a couple dozen one day and gorged ourselves. Eating a ripe mango and having the juice run down my hand and arm really takes me back to my childhood. I had about seven in a row and I had to skip dinner that night. They were so good it was hard to stop.

We tried another mall and I finally found a pair of boots I liked enough to buy. Later, Susie got her hair cut very short and permed. We spent that afternoon at the University of Zambia. There is a lake at the university which is ringed with willow trees and acacias. It is very peaceful and students often study there. We sat there for a couple hours, catching up on old times.

I still wanted to see Victoria Falls. I had seen it from Siavonga when I was a child. This time I wanted to see it from Livingstone. We looked at options to get to Livingstone: I could take a bus, fly or drive. Flights were more expensive than flying to another country, maybe because it was last minute and a popular destination. The disadvantages of taking a bus were that it would take a long time, and I would need to figure out transportation around Livingstone once I got there. Susie said she was game to come along so we decided to drive. I didn't have my international driver's license so that meant Susie would be driving the 7 hours to Livingstone by herself. I felt bad about that but with all the checkpoints along the way, it was the best thing to do.

Susie and I packed and loaded her car, then got on the road to Livingstone. It was the start of the rainy season so everything was green around us. We drove through Mazabuka, nicknamed the sweetest town in Zambia because of its sugar production. Trucks from Dangote, a popular Nigerian cement company, were plentiful on the road and I was impressed by Nigeria's reach. I had, of course, seen similar trucks in Cameroon but that was more expected since Nigeria and Cameroon are neighbors.

We only stopped once, in Choma, to grab lunch. We passed a lot of small villages along the way. It was gratifying to see primary and secondary schools at each one, a legacy of the first president, Dr. Kenneth Kaunda.

Seven hours later, we arrived in Livingstone and checked into our hotel. The grounds were beautiful with Koi ponds, flowers and greenery but we couldn't linger as we had to get to Victoria Falls. The hotel offered different tours but their prices were ridiculous. Besides, they weren't offering anything I hadn't done before: game drives, bungee jumping, etc. I just wanted to see the Falls.

Victoria Falls is also called Mosi-oa-Tunya, which means "the smoke that thunders." It is on the Zambezi River and lies on the border between Zambia and Zimbabwe. It is the largest waterfall in the world being 5,600 feet wide and

354 feet high.

We drove to the Falls and paid the entrance fee. Livingstone felt much hotter than Lusaka and I regretted wearing jeans *and* boots.

Victoria Falls or Mosi-oa-Tunya Falls

We wandered through the park, crossing the formidable Knife Edge Bridge. It was the start of the rainy season so the Falls were not yet at their peak, although they would be by April. They were still impressive. The advantage of seeing the Falls during off peak season is that one could see the cliffs that form the waterfall more clearly. There was less mist and spray to obscure the view.

Suddenly, it started to rain with lots of thunder and lightning. There was no humidity so the temperature immediately dropped by at least 15°F. We had been hot; we were now soaked to the skin and chilled to the bone. Susie was supposed to avoid getting her permed hair wet for forty eight hours but there was nothing we could do to keep it dry. We had no umbrella. We were lucky that my purse was waterproof so we could store my camera and our phones in it. My new boots were completely soaked. I didn't know if they would survive. The path was paved, so at least they weren't muddy.

Knife Edge Bridge

We started walking back to the bridge. I spotted a sign that explained the geology of the Falls. We walked on and about 10 minutes later, I spotted a similar sign. It occurred to me that it might be the same sign. We ended up wandering in circles trying to find our way back to shelter. Even plants and trees started to look familiar. It was raining heavily but it was the thunder and lightning that worried me.

Eventually we made it to the bridge and, of course, the rain petered out as we got to the other side. We had to laugh at ourselves. I hadn't been rained on this badly since I was a child. I was glad Susie took it so well. Her hair was ruined but her reaction was,

"Oh well, nothing we can do about it now."

She is such a cool, laid back person. I had had things go wrong on my trip but I realized a long time ago that holding on to things would rob me of my enjoyment. I chose my battles and went with the flow on everything else. That's part of what makes traveling fun, not knowing what will happen next.

We went to the top of the back of the Falls, which is impossible to do during peak season. We could see the mist rising up from the pounding water, which clearly explains why the waterfalls are called "the smoke that thunders."

Our next challenge was to hike down to Boiling Pot which is a permanent whirlpool on the Zambezi River. There was no paved path here although there are steps at the beginning of the hike. Sometimes, we found ourselves clambering over rocks and trees. On the way down, we were stalked by a baboon mother who had her baby clinging tightly to her. I happened to glance backwards and caught her following us. We made eye contact and we both stopped as we each tried to decide what to do next. Now, both Susie and I are on the short and skinny side. I could picture this baboon catching up to us and having her way with us. But when she noticed me noticing her, she stopped in her tracks. I continued hiking down but the next time I looked back, she was gone.

We made it down to Boiling Pot in about twenty minutes but it felt like an hour. The churning of the water was impressive to see. We could also see the Victoria Falls Bridge from there. We enjoyed the spot for a few minutes then turned to go back, as it was starting to get dark. We hiked back, still damp, and drove back to the hotel.

The hot shower I took that night felt like heaven, soothing my aching muscles. We had a wonderful dinner, savoring the bliss that comes from a day well-spent and filled with pleasant memories. Needless to say, we slept like logs that night under our mosquito nets.

The next day, we had breakfast and checked out of the hotel. I would have loved to see the Falls from the Zimbabwe side. Unfortunately, my passport had only 2 blank pages remaining. I knew I could get more pages added at the embassy in South Africa. If I went into Zimbabwe that day, I would need a page for when I returned to Zambia after viewing the Falls from the Zimbabwe side. Then I would have only one page remaining, assuming Zimbabwe's visa did not take up a whole page. One of the requirements to enter South Africa was to have at least 2 pages remaining in your passport. I didn't want to risk not being able to enter South Africa. That day, I found out about the UniVisa which allows entry into both Zambia and Zimbabwe. Unfortunately for me, on that day, it was not available at the Livingstone border. I decided to save my passport pages, just to be on the safe side.

I had a yearning to see hippos so on our way back to Lusaka, we stopped at Mosi-oa-Tunya National Park. We chose the road along the Zambezi River in hopes we would spot hippos in the river. Susie had a fantastic eye for distant wildlife. She spotted several hippos in the river but they were almost completely submerged. We finally spotted one on the bank close to the road. We got some pictures of him as he made his way back down to the river. We also saw giraffes, warthogs, zebra, impala, vervet monkeys and guinea fowl.

On our way out of the park, we happened upon a herd of Cape buffalo. They were on both sides of the road so we were essentially surrounded by them. To say they were menacing is an understatement. I have never understood the term "mean mugging" until that moment. I could sense the hostility emanating from them as they glared at us. Cape buffalo are part of the Big Five, the hardest animals to hunt. A guide once told me,

> "If you shoot a Cape buffalo, you better kill it. If you don't, it will come after you, find you, and kill you."

Looking at them now, I believed him. We took a few pictures then decided to leave while we still could.

Cape Buffalo

We drove on and spotted a family of elephants in the river. There were two adults and one calf and they were splashing about, seemingly having a great time. We must have surprised them because their reaction was to come out of the water and come after us. We didn't wait around to find out what would happen. Susie stepped on the gas and we pooled off. In fact, that was the last stop we made. The car we were driving would have been no match for the elephants, or even the Cape buffalo for that matter. We decided to head home and stop tempting fate.

We drove back to Lusaka, stopping in Choma to pick up snacks. We had a proper dinner when we got home. Poor Susie was exhausted from the long drive. We called it a night and turned in.

I didn't realize it at the time but Susie had a lot of firsts the week that I spent with them. She had never had Chinese food before, had never eaten with chopsticks, had never walked cheetahs. The drive to Livingstone was the longest she had ever done on her own. Even cutting her hair was an adventure. I didn't set out to change her life. I think in humoring me and being a good hostess, she had a great time herself and because she was open to the experiences, she learned a lot about her own inner strength. I learned a lot from traveling with her. I hope that I can be as good a companion to others as she was to me.

I left for Zimbabwe the next afternoon. I didn't want to leave but I had to let Susie get back to her life. She and the kids accompanied me to the airport and we parted after many hugs.

I ran into a soccer team from Egypt and made friends with some of them. Their flight left before mine so I posted pictures to Instagram while I waited for my flight. I sent some photos to Kibs and told her how much fun I was having.

Tips for travel to Zambia

- Make sure you have enough pages in your passport as the visa takes up a whole page.

- Consider getting the UniVisa, a visa which allows entry into both Zambia and Zimbabwe.

- Credit cards are not accepted everywhere so be sure to have cash on hand.

- If you visit Victoria (Mosi-oa-Tunya) Falls, take an umbrella or a parka so you don't get drenched if it rains. Carry waterproof bags for your cameras and phones.

Zimbabwe

Great Enclosure at the Great Zimbabwe ruins

The flight from Lusaka, Zambia to Harare, Zimbabwe took a little over an hour. I paid for a visa, which took up an entire page. My lodge sent a car to pick me up but I made sure to stop at the ATM at the airport first. I was able to get US dollars from the machine since that is the currency used in Zimbabwe at present.

I rode in the front as usual and chatted with the driver to get an idea of what to expect. On the way to the lodge, we passed Mukuvisi Woodlands, a game reserve conveniently located in Harare. I felt like I had had enough animal encounters in Zambia so I didn't add it to my list of things to do in Zimbabwe.

My driver and I were caught in rush hour traffic so we had plenty of time to chat. He was trained as a mechanic and was saving up to open his own shop. He said government policies were preventing foreign direct investment in Zimbabwe. Since white-owned farms were seized,

Zimbabwe's economy had declined and had never recovered. The economic decline was due to sanctions on Zimbabwe by the west. Few people could find work. Those who had jobs were in constant danger of being laid off.

Road leading from Harare airport

The last time I had been in Zimbabwe was in the mid-1990s. Back then Zimbabwe was still known as the breadbasket of Africa. Most people today are aware of the runaway inflation Zimbabwe has faced in the last decade, but few people know why. The present does not stand on its own. It requires history to give it context.

Zimbabwe gained independence after more than a decade of war with the British in 1980, about 20 years later than most other African countries. Zimbabwe's colonization history is unique. The British subjects who colonized the country were determined to wipe out the indigenous people. All wealth ended up in the hands of the British who only made up 3% of the population. The real owners of the land were forced on to reserves which had poor soil.

The British subjects in Zimbabwe issued the Unilateral Declaration of Independence (UDI) in 1965 which proclaimed their independence from Britain. Britain's reaction was a half-hearted attempt at sanctions which did not impact Zimbabwe much. In 1972, the UDI government made an agreement with Britain to allow majority Zimbabwean rule in the year 2015. The indigenous Zimbabweans, tired of being oppressed and seeing no end to the oppression, began guerrilla warfare on the UDI government, eventually gaining independence. Britain and the US committed to funding the purchase of white-owned farms which could then be redistributed. In the 1990s, Britain and the US reneged on the agreement and President Mugabe then started to take the farms back by force. We can debate the means taken by President Mugabe to right the wrongs set in motion by history. But we do him and Zimbabwe a disservice if we ignore the part played by British colonization.

Even though I was spending three nights in Zimbabwe, I was booked at my lodge for only one night. Most lodges, including the one where I was staying my first night, closed for Christmas and reopened after the new year. So, after the first night, I had to move to a lodge that remained open. Whereas the first lodge was excellent, the second lodge, although recommended by the first, was less than ideal. It wasn't horrible, but not up to my standards. I dealt with it since I had few options. At least they were accommodating.

The goal of my trip to Zimbabwe was to visit the Great Zimbabwe ruins which I had learned so much about in my high school history classes. My lodge helped me arrange a tour and after checking out the next morning, my driver and I set off for the ruins.

The name Zimbabwe is thought to mean either "houses of stone" or "venerated houses" in the Shona language. Great Zimbabwe is the largest of hundreds of such ruins found around Zimbabwe and the rest of southern Africa. Manyikeni in Mozambique is another well-known ruin. Great Zimbabwe is unusual because the houses were built with no mortar, similar to Machu Picchu in Peru. They are located near the city of Masvingo, about a 4 hour drive south from Harare.

We arrived at Great Zimbabwe and paid the entrance fee. I got a guide and we headed to the ruins. He was very knowledgeable and I enjoyed my tour with him.

As with most stone ruins, the real age is difficult to determine but it is estimated that the earliest settlement around Great Zimbabwe was in the 5th Century A.D., with continuous occupation between the 11th and 15th Century A.D. The walls range from 4 feet to 17 feet thick, and were as high as 36 feet. The ruins cover an area of roughly 1,800 acres and housed up to 18,000 people at their peak. Great Zimbabwe developed as a result of trade with the Middle East, West Africa, and the Far East. Its chief export was most likely gold. Soapstone birds found around the ruins, thought to be fish eagles, were added to Zimbabwe's flag after independence.

The colonial regime refused to acknowledge that the ruins had been built by Africans, alleging instead that they were the product of European influence. Archeological evidence has proven that indigenous Africans developed this massive stone city.

Great Zimbabwe comprises three parts: the Hill Complex, the Valley Complex and the Great Enclosure. My guide and I started with the Hill Complex. The Hill ruins were built around granite mounds on a hill. From a distance, the Hill Ruins are almost indistinguishable from the mounds, providing excellent camouflage and protection from enemies. The king was thought to live in the Hill Complex.

My guide climbing to the Hill Complex

The Great Enclosure is where the wives of the kings lived. Outside of the Great Enclosure lie the Valley ruins, where everyone else lived. The Conical Tower is found here but its purpose is unknown. It is 33 feet high and 16 feet in diameter. The dentelle decoration at the top was destroyed by Karl Mauch in 1871 as he sought treasure in the non-existent hollow interior.

It is speculated that Great Zimbabwe declined as a result of decreasing soil fertility and quality. The splitting away of one of the princes, Nyatsimba Mutota, around 1430 to create the Mwene Mutapa empire in the north, is thought to have also contributed to Great Zimbabwe's decline. The creation of the Kingdom of Butua to the south likely also had an impact on Great Zimbabwe.

The day was bright, sunny and hot. If visiting in the hot season, I recommend starting early in the morning, instead of at noon like I did. On the other hand, the sun made the colors appear very intense. Only in Africa is the sky so blue.

Fluffums and I in front of the Conical Tower

It easily took three hours for us to go through all of the ruins. The Hill ruins are much bigger than they appear from the outside. Some of the walls were deliberately built so narrow that only one person can fit through at a time. This was done so that attackers could easily be disarmed.

FROM ANTARCTICA TO ZIMBABWE

Visiting Great Zimbabwe was a dream come true for me. The ruins were more impressive than I could have dreamed. It's incredible that structures built so long ago could still exist today. I cast my mind back to Stonehenge and Machu Picchu. I guess you could say stone is forever.

As we drove back to Harare, my driver told me of other interesting things to do near Harare. One option was hiking Mount Nyangani, Zimbabwe's highest mountain at 8,504 feet. It was four hours east of Harare though. I didn't think I could take much more driving. What's interesting about the mountain is that people disappear on it all the time, similar to the Bermuda Triangle. I brought this up to my driver and he said the best way to be safe on the mountain was to keep silent if I saw anything strange.

The Chinhoyi Caves were another option. They are made of limestone and house a remarkable pool of cobalt blue water. I seriously considered visiting these caves but at two hours away from Harare, they were still farther than I wanted to travel. Remember that I had spent the prior days driving to and from Livingstone, then traveling to Harare, and now driving eight hours to and from Masvingo. To say I was tired would be an understatement. I decided to use my last day in Harare to just rest and relax.

On the drive back to Harare, we passed many trucks and buses traveling to and from South Africa. There were a few police checkpoints checking for driver's license and car registration. They also had a "Drive To Arrive Alive" campaign going on and the police reminded people to drive carefully. It was only two days to Christmas. Many people in Zimbabwe return to their home village for

Christmas so there were many cars on the road. As in other African countries I had visited thus far, motorists signaled each other to warn of upcoming checkpoints.

I asked my driver about the state of affairs in Zimbabwe. In his opinion, things were going fine. He appeared to have no complaints.

I spent my last day in Zimbabwe doing absolutely nothing. I was exhausted to the bone. After I woke up, I stayed in bed, watching TV. It was 11 am before I finally had the strength to take a shower and go to breakfast. I lounged some more until dinner time. I was incredibly refreshed by the end of the day.

The next day, I left for the airport around noon. I rode with my third driver in Zimbabwe. His opinion of the economy was that things were getting better and the economy was improving. He mentioned that a lot of Zimbabweans in the diaspora were returning to the country and investing in it. I was cheered by his optimism. How interesting, though, that all three drivers gave me a different opinion. I wonder where the truth lies.

I got through immigration with no issues. I was flying to Cape Town via Johannesburg. A young, white Zimbabwean started chatting with me, and kept me entertained until the flight left. She was fifteen and heading to Johannesburg to join her father for the holidays. Her stories of a broken family were truly sad and I felt for her, traveling from one country to another to spend time with each parent. She wanted to be a fashion designer when she grew up. I checked out her designs and they were actually really good. Hopefully, her dreams will come true.

She told me of her travels to Lesotho, which was on my list as well. Lesotho is known for skiing in the winter. It was the hot season so I knew the snow would be gone, but she assured me the mountains were high enough that some snow would remain. Thus encouraged, I kept Lesotho on my list.

Tower at Harare airport designed like Conical Tower at Great Zimbabwe

The flight was over an hour late leaving Harare. That meant we arrived late in Johannesburg, also affectionately known as Joburg or Jozi. After getting through immigration and security, I saw that my flight to Cape Town was to board soon. I ran through the airport and made the flight by the skin of my teeth. I had no service on the plane obviously, so I borrowed a phone to call Kibs and let her know I made the flight. Then I sat back and caught my breath. The older couple sitting next to me were very polite to each other. They said "thanks very much" and "please" to each other. It was very nice to see.

Tips for travel to Zimbabwe

- Ensure you have a whole passport page for Zimbabwean visa.

- US dollars are widely used. Carry small notes.

- Consider getting the UniVisa, a visa which allows entry into both Zambia and Zimbabwe. That will allow you to see Victoria Falls (Mosi-oa-Tunya) from both countries without paying extra.

- I found that tours were difficult to book online. Ask your hotel to help you set up tours before your arrival.

South Africa

Table Mountain in Cape Town

My dear friend Kibs was at Cape Town International Airport to pick me up. After hugs and greetings, we walked to the parking garage. It was really good to see her even though it had only been a couple of months since we last saw each other. It was Christmas Eve and Kibs was hosting a dinner that night. Since it was already after 8 pm, we hurried back to the apartment Kibs shared with her boyfriend, Daniel. We had never met but I'd heard plenty of good things about him.

We arrived at the apartment and I was introduced to Daniel and the dinner guests. Daniel was just as Kibs had described, a nice guy with a great sense of humor. He and Kibs went to the kitchen and the rest of us chatted and got to know each other better.

Dinner was served and it was a veritable feast. There was an enormous ham, gravy, chapati, pickled cabbage, pilau rice and stewed greens. We ate and drank and made merry. It was very late by the time the last guest left. I was exhausted. We went to bed and I slept late into the next morning.

Over the next few days, I caught up with Kibs. I shared my experiences on the trip with her. She shared what was going on in her life. She had some major issues going on and I listened sympathetically. I had no idea how to fix her problems but I offered advice where I could. A lot of it required just allowing time to pass.

I noticed that Kibs was really short with everyone. She is normally the nicest person you'll ever meet so I chalked it up to her being stressed out. I figured I could help my friend the way I was helping myself, by taking her away for a few days. The distance from her problems would hopefully give her perspective and allow her to find herself again. This trip was different from any I had ever taken before. I could feel myself changing. While I'm normally extremely cautious, I was opening up to being more adventurous with my life choices. More importantly, I was less willing to settle for less than what I actually wanted out of life. I wanted Kibs to get some kind of epiphany about her own life.

I brought the idea to her, and offered to pay for the trip. She accepted immediately and we started planning. She was like a sister to me, so I didn't think twice about spending any money on her.

Around this time, I noticed she was constantly WhatsApp'ing, and most of the time it was not for business. I remembered all of my messages she hadn't replied to and I felt so confused. I had thought she was too busy to respond to me, yet here she was sending and receiving nonsense videos at all hours of the day and night. Then why hadn't she responded to my messages? I tucked that away in the back of my mind.

Cape Town is an amazing city. This was my fourth visit so I didn't feel the need to do all the touristy things again. This was more about spending time with Kibs. If you travel to Cape Town, I recommend going to the top of Table Mountain by cable car; going to Stellenbosch, the wine country outside of the city; visiting Robben Island where Nelson Mandela was kept prisoner; going on game drives; going to the southernmost tip of Africa, Cape Agulhas; visiting the Cape of Good Hope where the Dutch first landed in 1652; driving to Simon's Town to see the penguins; and driving along the Garden Route, enjoying the mountain and ocean scenery and the myriad quaint little towns along the way. Regarding activities, one can buy art from Green Market Square; go parasailing; dive with the sharks; or bungee jumping off Bloukrans Bridge, the highest bungee in the world. There is something for everyone.

Daniel suggested visiting Hermanus for whale watching. It was not whale season but we decided to go anyway. The drive was beautiful with the mountains on one side and the blue ocean on the other. At Daniel's suggestion, we stopped first at Betty's Bay to see African penguins.

We spent a couple hours at Betty's Bay, simply enjoying the sunny weather, the magnificent views and the penguins. The colony of African Penguins was very large and spread over a big area. There were many penguins moulting or shedding and regrowing their feathers. Just like in Antarctica, cormorants could also be seen nearby.

These cormorants were jet black unlike the white and grey ones in Antarctica.

Shipwreck and penguins at Betty's Bay

We left reluctantly and headed to Hermanus. On the way, we inadvertently found ourselves in a luxury car convoy, and we drove along with them as far as we could. Ferraris and Lamborghinis were plentiful around us. People were lined up along the route so it must have been for a well-publicized event. Their confused faces were priceless as we passed them in our humble car and waved like we were royalty.

On the drive, Daniel mentioned quaggas, which are a now-extinct species of zebra. The front of it had brown and white stripes, while the rear was brown like a horse. The quagga was hunted to extinction, with the last known specimen dying in a zoo in 1883. I looked at Daniel in amazement, sure that he was making it all up. It took a lot for him to convince me because I had never heard of quaggas in my life. I wondered what else was lost to us forever, that I would never even know about.

African penguin at Betty's Bay

We got to Hermanus in the early afternoon. Unfortunately, we spotted no whales but we did have an excellent lunch at a restaurant near the ocean. Hermanus is a beautiful little city and very picturesque. We took a walk after lunch, just taking it all in. We found a restaurant that had a board on the outside of it that read,

> "Before I die, I want to..."

and there were blanks for people to fill in. Some of the answers were lofty,

> "Before I die, I want to see world peace."

Others were sweet,

"Before I die, I want to kiss Kristi."

Others were unexpected,

"Before I die, I want to become a nice dictator"

My favorite was,

"Before I die, I want to do what makes me happy."

The most important thing I had to do in Cape Town was to get pages added to my passport. For that, I would have to go to the US Embassy. I booked an appointment and told Kibs I would take a cab. She insisted on taking me, so we went together. It was a disaster. My appointment took a few hours since the passport machine was being repaired. Kibs waited outside the embassy, and worked on her laptop. She became impatient when her battery ran out and started sending messages to me through the security guards. Every few minutes, the guards would come to me and tell me she wanted me to go outside and meet her. I was in shock at her behavior. After the umpteenth time the guard approached me, I went to one of the people processing passports and asked how much longer my passport would take. I hated being put in that position. I consider myself a reasonable person; when it was first explained to me that the machine was being repaired, I understood that I would have to wait an hour or two. I had no problem with that. No electronics are allowed at the embassy so I couldn't call Kibs and let her know. But that shouldn't have been a problem; I wasn't playing games or hanging out. If I was still in there, it had to be for a good reason.

This incident really made me concerned for my friend. Her behavior was out of control. It made me think her issues must be worse than I had thought.

We found a hair salon and they did an excellent job of rebraiding my hair. Now I could focus on planning the next phase of my trip. I decided that I wanted to go to Namibia, Lesotho, Swaziland and Mozambique.

Kibs made most of the arrangements for us. I was skeptical but I let it happen. I felt she needed to make the arrangements so she could feel better about herself. I hoped I wouldn't regret it. We bought flights to Walvis Bay, Namibia and packed our bags, and said goodbye to Daniel. I was now on a quest to save my friend.

Tips for travel to South Africa

- Ensure you have at least 2 blank passport pages or entry could be denied.

- If visiting at Christmas/New Year's, book activities well in advance as they tend to be sold out.

- Credit cards are used widely so no need to carry a lot of cash.

- You may need an electric outlet adaptor not available in most other countries. It has three large circular prongs in a triangular formation.

Namibia

Fluffikins at Deadvlei in Sossusvlei

Kibs and I arrived at Walvis Bay Airport in Namibia around 5 pm. We were supposed to pick up a rental car at the airport. To our amazement, the rental car company was closed when we got to their office. We were able to borrow a phone from an airport employee and call the rental company. They claimed to have no record of our reservation. What was worse was that they had no cars left. I have to admit that I believed the car company over Kibs, knowing that anytime she set something up for me, it never went well. Since we had not paid a deposit, I suggested renting from another company but Kibs insisted she could get them to resolve the issue. She would get them to bring a car to us by the following morning. Meanwhile, our new friend, the airport employee, called a cab for us and we headed to our guesthouse in Swakopmund.

The drive to the guesthouse took about twenty minutes. It

was very scenic, with the desert on one side and the Atlantic Ocean on the other, the ships on the ocean, and the colorful houses on the beach. The guesthouse itself was lovely; our room was spacious with a balcony that opened to the garden.

We were in Namibia primarily because I wanted to go sand-boarding in the Namib Desert. Kibs had found a tour company that would take us sand-boarding the day after we arrived. Afterwards, we would drive to Sossusvlei to see the highest sand dune in Namibia. I had been looking forward to sand-boarding since South America. In fact, I had been wanting to sand-board for years. I couldn't wait.

Dinner was a quiet affair. I was struggling to find the words to tell Kibs she was not behaving appropriately. On the trip from Cape Town to Walvis Bay, she had been really short with everyone we interacted with. I had seen what effects stress can have on people during my last year with Big Oil Co. Knowing Kibs for as long as I have, I knew this was not who she was. I finally found some words, and I told her I knew she was going through a tough time, but everything would eventually work out. I reminded her that the trip was an opportunity for her to let loose and open up, and forget about her problems for a few days. Finally, I asked her to be kinder to people we met, especially as we were travelers. I brought up some examples of inappropriate interactions she'd had with Daniel in front of me. She listened in silence, and agreed to be nicer, but I could tell her feelings were hurt. I hurt for her because I could tell she felt like she was losing control of her circumstances and herself. Dinner became even quieter.

The following morning, Kibs spent hours on the phone with the car rental company. They did not have any cars, and so couldn't bring one to us that morning. Kibs insisted that they find one and bring it to us even if it had to be brought from another city. Eventually, they agreed. But by then we were late for our sand-boarding activity. Our guide waited 30 minutes for us. I was embarrassed because I hate wasting other people's time. I was even more embarrassed when I realized the guide had to stop at other lodges and pick up tourists who had been waiting on us.

As far as I was concerned, that car rental company was a lost cause. We had not actually spent any money with them so we could cut our losses and move on to another company. Time is of the essence during travel. Sometimes, it is more valuable than money. I started to see that time didn't matter to Kibs as much as it did to me.

We arrived at the dunes and were briefed on how the day would go. We could sand-board standing or lying down, although everyone would get the opportunity to sand-board lying down. I chose stand up boarding, of course, so I could do both. The company provided all the gear we needed, and training as well. We started around 10:30 am and finished around 2 pm. It was exhilarating and exhausting. Climbing back up the dunes after boarding down really took a lot out of us, and the heat wasn't helping. I fell many times but the sand didn't hurt so it was still great fun. Despite my inexperience, I did some jumps off the board that was set up. Although I fell on each jump, I improved every time, and I was much better by the third jump.

The lie-down boarding required one to lie down on the board on one's stomach, hold up the front edge of the board, and enjoy the ride down the dunes. There was much screaming and a lot of sand but it was very enjoyable. Days later, I was still finding sand in all manner of crevices. Sand fell out of my hair for weeks afterwards.

Sand-boarding in the Namib Desert near Swakopmund

Kibs spent a lot of time on the phone with the rental company and only made it down the big slope once, as we ended the day and headed back to the cars. The sight of her sitting on the dunes, arguing with the car company on the guide's phone, wasting away the money I had spent on the activity made me very angry. I fought hard and pushed that emotion away, because I was living one of my dreams, and I wanted to get the most out of it. I made a choice to enjoy myself with or without her. If she didn't want peace in her life, I couldn't force it on her. It had taken me months to find my own peace. I realized I might be rushing her. Kibs clearly wasn't ready. I realized

You can't save everyone.

It's even possible that you can't save anyone and we all have to save ourselves. I would do my best to facilitate things but she had to make her own way there. I decided,

"F*@# this sh*t."

I stopped trying to include her and focused on myself. I

had a much more enjoyable time.

At the end, we were provided a light lunch and the most welcome cold drinks I've ever had. Around this time, our rental car showed up. We had to drive the driver back so we missed the ending ceremony where everyone was handed their certificates. I started to miss traveling solo, but I remained patient, telling myself my friend needed me.

We were covered in sand so we needed to take showers. Unfortunately, we had already checked out of our room. Luckily for us, the guesthouse owner was very accommodating and let us use his room to clean up. Afterwards, we stopped at a supermarket for snacks and drinks. Then we started the drive to Sossusvlei.

The drive to Sossusvlei was incredibly scenic. It was flat for the most part, occasionally interrupted by mountains. There was very sparse vegetation, and we sometimes guessed at the location of underground streams when we saw green trees growing in a line. We sang aloud to music, talked about old times and thoroughly enjoyed ourselves. Kibs was in a much better mood since she had triumphed over the rental company. She drove first, for about 2 hours, then I took over. The road changed from tar to gravel after a couple hours. The roads are gravel to preserve the unique ecosystem in that part of the country. The drive was supposed to take four and a half hours but it was five and a half hours before we got to Sossusvlei.

We ran into a couple whose car had broken down. They were heading in the opposite direction, to Swakopmund. The woman was ill and they had been waiting for five hours for roadside assistance from the rental car company, which was supposed to have shown up two hours prior. This was the same rental company we had been dealing with. There was no cellphone service available as we were driving through mountains, so they couldn't call for help. There are no emergency shelters or phones along the way so we offered to call for help as soon as we got to our lodge. We gave them a bottle of water and some snacks. Then we took their information as well as their contact at the car rental company so we could make sure they were rescued.

View on the drive to Sossusvlei

The couple told us that several other people had stopped to help them, and had promised to call on their behalf as soon as they got cellphone service. I glanced at their back seat and saw that they had several bottles of water in their car and I was so glad that others had also stopped to help them. When we got to our lodge, we called the rental car company and they assured us they had been rescued.

DR. QUINTA

We actually ran into the couple a few days later at the airport in Windhoek on our way to Johannesburg. They said they weren't rescued until an hour and a half after we left them. This experience shook me up quite a bit as I realized we were not prepared for the isolated terrain. This is another reason I prefer to use guides especially if my stay is short. It's impossible to know everything about a new place. The isolation on the road and the lack of emergency services were not something I had expected. As we drove off, I hoped fervently that we wouldn't need help ourselves.

Driving on gravel is tricky and, at first, I had to fight to keep the car from sliding around. I found that by slowing down, I could keep the car under better control. I slowed down even more when we drove through mountain passes, trying to keep the SUV from going over the edge.

We finally showed up at our lodge in Sossusvlei at about 8 pm. Fortunately, dinner was still being served. We ate and turned in for the night. The following morning, I stayed in bed, reading *Americanah* by Chimamanda Adichie. I had borrowed it from Kibs' library in Cape Town. I needed the rest as my body felt broken with exhaustion from sand-boarding in the hot desert sun, as well as the long drive. Kibs started planning the next leg of the trip.

Kibs and I were both coughing and, remembering my experience in the Sahara, I attributed it to the sand from the desert getting into our lungs. Luckily, I still had the medicine my sister had prescribed for me. I shared it with Kibs.

That morning, for the first time in five years, it rained in Sossusvlei. Light rain pattered for the rest of the day, all night and the following morning as well. I was glad to experience another first on my trip around the world.

Sossus means "dead end" in the Nama language, while *vlei*, pronounced flay, means marsh in Afrikaans. When there is enough rain, the nearby Tsauchab River fills the clay pan, creating a glassy lake which reflects the surrounding dunes.

It was New Year's Eve. At midnight, we called, WhatsApp'ed, emailed, and Facebooked our loved ones but we did nothing special to commemorate the day. I simply had no energy and Kibs seemed content to laze about with me. I made some resolutions, the most important being along the lines of not being afraid to go for what I want.

The next day, we went on a guided tour of the area. Our first stop was Sesriem Canyon, which was formed by the activity of the Tsauchab River. *Sesriem* means "six ropes" in Afrikaans and refers to the ropes that were used in years past to pull water from the canyon. The canyon and rock formations around it were beautiful. I marveled at the power of water to cut through rock.

We had a light breakfast next to the canyon before we moved on to the next site. The next stop was Dune 45, so named because it is 45 km from Sesriem Gate. It is one of the highest dunes in Namibia at roughly 600 feet, the highest dunes being almost 1,000 feet high. Namibia is said to have the highest dunes in the world, and the Namib Desert is said to be the oldest in the world. The red sand is due to a high content of iron oxide, while the black accents are due to unoxidized iron. I was filled with horror when our guide told us later that several snakes, including side winders, pythons and horn adders, can be found on the dunes.

It was easily 10 am when we started to climb the dunes, and it was already very hot. I took my shoes off so I could climb easier, but left my socks on so the hot sand would not blister my feet. The view from the dune was incredible. We could see blue skies, distant purple dunes and closer red and pink dunes. The dunes are distinct and easy to recognize. I was watching the remake of *Mad Max* a year later and I could tell part of it was filmed in the Namib Desert.

Sitting on Dune 45 in Sossusvlei

I recommend climbing early in the morning, before sunrise if possible. By the time we came back down, we were parched. I thought of the Sahara and I was glad I had visited the Sahara during the winter. I couldn't imagine spending hours sitting on Dune 45 this time of year. It was much too hot. Coming back down was easier than climbing. I ran down the steep side of the dune as fast as I could. It was a fun and strange sensation because the sand held my feet and kept me from falling over. Our guide had bottles of water waiting for us when we came back down, though they were not cold. We gulped them down anyway.

Our last stop was Deadvlei. I recommend not self-driving as the road to Deadvlei is a dry river bed. It's easy to get stuck or run into rocks hidden under the sand. Deadvlei, meaning "dead marsh," is a clay pan full of dead trees. The trees are thought to have died from lack of water almost 1,000 years ago. It was so dry that the trees could not even decompose. So their carcasses stand, scorched and stark against the white, salt-covered clay, like something on an alien planet. It is quite beautiful with the red dunes behind it. At this time of day, however, we were exposed to the scorching sun. It was about 104°F at Deadvlei. Walking almost 1 mile from the car park to the vlei through the sand was difficult. After taking enough pictures, we headed back to the car. I felt like throwing up and I knew this was a sign of approaching heat stroke. Fortunately, we got to the car in time and got some much needed water.

Our guide told us of the Namibia Alien, a creature that was caught and killed in 2013. It looked like a cross between a man and a rabbit. Not much has been heard since the body was taken away to be autopsied by the CIA. This was the first time I was hearing about it and I was shocked. He made it seem like common knowledge in Namibia. I later searched online and I did find reports and pictures of it. In this day and age though, who knows what pictures are actually real. I really want the story to be true.

We returned to the lodge and took showers and changed. Then we packed up and left for Windhoek. We were flying to Durban, South Africa via Johannesburg the next day. From Durban, we would make our way to Lesotho.

Windhoek at night

The five hour drive was very enjoyable with scenic views and fun conversation. Kibs drove for about an hour and I took over. The drive was so much fun this time. Our guide had taught us how to drive on gravel. Apparently, the trick is to drive very fast and make small corrections if the car drifts. Driving that way was so much fun that when the road changed to tar, I got bored and handed the car back to Kibs. I finally understood why people like to go off-roading.

It was dark when we arrived in Windhoek. It appeared beautiful even at night with Christmas decorations lighting up the streets. We checked into our hotel and had dinner. Kibs appeared much more relaxed and I was really happy to see her enjoying herself at last.

Overall, I enjoyed Namibia tremendously. I recommend traveling there towards the end of the cool season since most activities take place in the desert. The food was never bad but never great either. The people are hard to describe. They are not unfriendly but nothing stood out about them. Still, I did enjoy myself and we were treated well wherever we went.

We were up early to catch our flight to Johannesburg. Traveling to Botswana next had been an option but hotel prices were astronomical this time of year. We drove to the airport and dropped off the rental car. The flight to Joburg was uneventful. We had to go through immigration in Joburg and I was delayed because the officer was hitting on me. I took it in stride, chatted politely and accepted his number when he offered it. By the time he let me through, the other passengers were long gone. Fortunately, we had a long layover so we didn't have to run to make the next flight.

We grabbed coffee then headed to our gate. We got to Durban in no time.

Tips for travel to Namibia

- If driving, ensure you have a working cell phone, emergency food and water, and a first aid kit

- Due to the desert terrain and isolated nature of some parts of the country, I recommend using a local guide

- If you are not comfortable driving on gravel, hire a driver.

- Do not climb dunes with your bare feet. The heat will blister your soles.

Lesotho

At the border between South Africa and Lesotho

We picked up our rental car at King Shaka International Airport in Durban and drove to our Airbnb apartment. The apartment was near uShaka Beach. Before we had dinner, I met up with a high school classmate, Lionel, whose office happened to be nearby. Later, all three of us walked to the Waterfront at uShaka Beach for dinner. The area was beautiful. There were condos built around a canal, and gondolas on the canal. Once we got to the Waterfront, there were various restaurants and shops, and an aquarium. Quite a few activities are available including swimming with dolphins and diving with sharks. Even though it was nighttime, there were a lot of people in the area. We picked a restaurant that was built into an old shipwreck and had a lovely dinner.

The next morning, we had a day tour to the country of Lesotho. We drove west to the tour office in Underberg. We got lost once or twice, but we still made it there on time.

Lesotho is a country completely surrounded by South Africa. It developed that way because the country was founded by Bushmen and Nguni tribesmen escaping the Mfecane wars waged by Shaka Zulu, my favorite person in history. To digress a little, Shaka Zulu's wars in the early 1800s caused movement of people north from South Africa into the areas that are now Zimbabwe, Zambia, Mozambique, Tanzania and all the way north into Uganda and Kenya. This is why some languages in these countries are similar. Shaka Zulu was the illegitimate child of a prince. Though his early life was challenging, he overcame that and eventually became king of the Zulus. He was such a force that he reshaped the populations around southern Africa. That is why he is one of my heroes.

The Kingdom of Lesotho is very mountainous and its highest point is at 11,400 feet. In the winter, the mountains are snow covered and skiing takes place on the slopes. Temperatures often fall below 0°F in the winter. Sadly for me, it was summer so all the snow had melted. I thought back to the young lady I met at Harare International Airport who told me I could see the snow all year round. She must have gotten her seasons mixed up.

The drive to Lesotho took us through the majestic Drakensburg Mountains. Occasionally, we would spot birds and other wildlife. Our guide was excellent and stopped often to give us background information and the opportunity to take photos. We drove to the South African border at Sani Pass, then continued to the Lesotho border where we got both our entry and exit visas.

The drive through Sani Pass was bumpy as the road is not tarred. Once in Lesotho, however, the road is tarred. Some parts of the pass had interesting names. Grace Corner was so named because in the winter, one passed there safely by the grace of god. Ice Corner was so named because the water cascading there froze in the winter.

Fluffy in the Drakensburg Mountains

The Drakensburg Mountains form a natural barrier between South Africa and Lesotho. Once you cross the border into Lesotho, another mountain range emerges, the Maluti Mountains. We were so high up that it became quite chilly and we had to don sweaters.

After entering Lesotho, we drove for a while and saw plenty of sheep grazing. We stopped at a settlement about twenty minutes from the border. The huts making up the settlement were built of stone and mortar. The roofs were made of grass and angled to prevent rain coming through. We entered a hut and the guide and a young lady from the settlement showed us various items that play a part in everyday life in the settlement. There were blankets, baskets and hats woven in Lesotho, and delicious fresh bread baked over a fire. The young lady showed us how to grind wheat by hand into flour. We tried it and it requires quite a bit of energy, as well as technique.

Animal husbandry is very important in Lesotho. Mohair, wool and water are some of the main exports.

Me dressed in traditional Lesotho attire

Afterwards we returned to Sani Pass and had lunch at the highest pub in Africa, which is at 9,430 feet. We sat at a table outside, looking down into the valley. I had a delicious stewed lamb. While we were eating, a group of Italian bikers came into the pub. They were exploring the country by bike. I wish we had more time to chat with them because I wonder about the logistics of traveling with their bikes. They recommended I visit Bergamo next time I was in Italy.

We drove back to Durban from Underberg, avoiding the cows in the road along the way. It was our last night in Durban so we went to the Waterfront one more time for dinner. The area was so quiet and beautiful. I wished we could stay longer.

The next morning, we had breakfast with Lionel at a nearby hotel. I really enjoyed hearing about his life. He had had multiple careers and they were all so different on the surface. That is an ideal way to live for me as I prefer breadth of experience to narrow depth. It was with much reluctance that I parted ways with him. If I had been alone, I would have definitely extended my stay in Durban. Durban itself was also a really cool city. The waterfront area in particular was quite beautiful. Kibs was just as surprised as I was, and I was disappointed in her for I believe a travel consultant should at least know what is good to do in her own country. She constantly talked up Cape Town, which I love, but downplayed every other part of the country. I vowed to return to Durban someday and enjoy the activities and cultural experiences available.

Our next destination was Manzini, Swaziland but we were stopping in St. Lucia, South Africa first. I still really wanted to see hippos and Kibs assured me that St. Lucia was a good place to see them. When we arrived in St. Lucia, we stopped at iSimangaliso Park center close to the edge of town. We stood on a bridge overlooking a river with hippos in it. There were a number of hippos in the river, although they remained submerged for the most part.

Hippos in St. Lucia, South Africa

We took pictures for a while then left. I was disappointed as I had thought we would be able to get on the river and see the hippos up close. As we were leaving, we saw a boat filled with tourists cruise up the river. It just drove home my disappointment. That was what I thought Kibs had planned for us. Frankly, Susie had done much better at the reserve in Zambia, and she wasn't even a travel consultant.

Almost as interesting as the hippos, was the strange art that was displayed at the center. There was a wire crocodile sculpture with the head of a man in its jaws. It was freaky but less nightmare-inducing than the sculpture that was a winged man with the head of a lion and the feet of a chicken on one side, and a winged man with exposed genitals and webbed feet on the other side. We shuddered and left St. Lucia.

We headed to the Swaziland border which was called Golela on the South African side and Lavumisa on the

Swaziland side.

Tips for travel to Lesotho

- Take warm clothes as the mountains make the weather unpredictable.

- Take plenty of cash for souvenirs.

- The South African Rand is widely accepted in Lesotho so no need to change money if you already have Rands.

- It is possible to fly from various cities in South Africa to Lesotho rather than by car.

Swaziland

View from our hotel dining room in Manzini

The Kingdom of Swaziland is a small country surrounded by South Africa to the north, west and south, and Mozambique to the east. The current ruler is King Mswati III.

We arrived at the border, my third land border crossing ever. We left South Africa with no problem. On the Lesotho side, we had to show proof that our rental car was not stolen. Fortunately, Kibs had remembered to get the necessary paperwork from the rental car company so we got through with no problem.

One of the immigration agents taught us that *Unjani* means hello in Swazi, and the appropriate response is *Nyapila*. In Zulu, one would say *Sawubona* and the response would be *Yebo*. We didn't use this information much as everyone we interacted with spoke English.

We left the Lavumisa border and headed northwest to Manzini. It was dark already so it was difficult to see anything. We got lost several times which was frustrating since it was night and we were tired. I wished I had insisted on the GPS. We eventually reached our lodge in Manzini around midnight. It was a lovely place, simple but very clean. We took showers and passed out.

When we went to breakfast the following morning, we were blown away by the view from the dining room. The colors were so intense, and the beautiful flowers and greenery, and a mountain made breakfast very enjoyable. Breakfast itself was excellent and the service was very good. Swazis, in my experience, are very nice people. The women, in particular, always greeted us by saying,

> "Hello, sister,"

which was nice and made us feel at home. We didn't change any money to Lilangeni as we found that Swaziland accepts the South African Rand. We used the Rand everywhere, even at filling stations.

We got back on the road after breakfast, heading for the Mozambican capital of Maputo. The day was hot and scorching, around 95°F, but the bright sunlight made for pretty views and a pleasant drive. There were a lot of cows on the hillsides and sometimes on the road as well. Potatoes, sweet potatoes, wood, and more were for sale on the side of road. We saw a lot of schools and training colleges along the way. I was particularly gratified to see a high school for the deaf not far from the new King Mswati III airport.

We got a little lost again since we had no cell service and

could not re-access Google Maps, but we were able to follow signs for the Lomasha border. We drove through Simunye which is famous for the Hlane Game Reserve and sugarcane fields. We saw amarula plants and I learned from Kibs that elephants eat the plants and become inebriated. The thought of drunken elephants really cracked me up.

Billboard against corruption in Swaziland

There were rolling hills all around us but as we got closer to the border, we noticed the remarkable Lebombo Mountains in front of us. We crossed Lomahasha into Namaacha on the Mozambican side.

Tips for travel to Swaziland

- If driving across borders, you need documents for your car to prove it is not stolen. Rental companies will provide the documents upon request.

- Bring GPS if driving. Although it's a small country, taking a wrong turn can add considerable delay to your trip.

- The South African Rand is accepted in Swaziland.

- Show respect for the King at all times.

Mozambique

View of Maputo from hotel balcony

We crossed from Lomasha, Swaziland into Namaacha, Mozambique. Maybe because of the mountain border, Mozambique looks completely different from the rolling hills of Swaziland. We stopped by the side of the road to buy some juicy looking mangoes that caught our eyes. We had no Metical, which is Mozambican currency, but the vendor kindly accepted our Rands. We drove on to Maputo.

Mozambique is one of a handful of countries in Africa where the official language is Portuguese. The others are Angola, Guinea Bissau, Equatorial Guinea, São Tomé and Principe, and Cape Verde Islands. I would have to remember the scant Portuguese I learned on my last trip to Brazil. My favorite Portuguese phrase is

Você fala Inglês? Do you speak English?

I usually have to resort to my not-so-great Spanish because I know very little Portuguese.

Our hotel was fairly new with a few parking spaces in front. We parked our car and checked in. Our room was high up and had a balcony with a fantastic view of Maputo. Maputo is the capital city and lies on the Indian Ocean coast. We had a fresh seafood dinner at our hotel and it was delicious.

Kibs was very short with the hotel staff. I sighed wearily. I just knew if there was a fire at the hotel, we would be left to burn to our deaths.

We spent the next day walking around the city and taking it all in. Some of the street names were names of famous communists, e.g. Avenida Karl Marx. A lot of them also paid tribute to other African countries and their leaders, for instance Avenida Kenneth Kaunda, named after the first president of Zambia.

Maputo is known as the "city of acacias." True to its name, the streets were lined with acacias, leafy and blooming with their characteristic red flowers. They provided much welcome shade from the blazing sun as we strolled through the city.

We stopped at the Maputo Shopping Centre for a light lunch. We sat at a table outside, resting our feet, and watching people go by. Ripped jeans were definitely in style and I lost count of the number of women who walked by wearing them. The mood was tranquil and I truly enjoyed myself that day. Simply walking around the city and absorbing the atmosphere was enough for me.

We came across the Maputo Fortress, which is now a museum and we entered and paid the entrance fee. There wasn't much to see but it was there that I learned of Ngungunyane, who was the last emperor of Gaza, which covered western Mozambique and southeastern Zimbabwe.

Street lined with acacias

We left the fort and after more walking, found ourselves at the ferry landing. We had no established plan but I really wanted to go to one of the islands off the mainland. We inquired from some of the officials and were taken to a private tour company that could rent us a boat and driver. The reason I preferred private over the public ferry was because I wanted flexibility over our schedule. The ferry left at 6 am and returned at 3 pm. With our own boat, we would be able to make multiple stops and leave when we were ready. We booked the last available boat and arranged to be picked up from our hotel the following morning.

We were quite hungry at this time so we stopped for

dinner at the Waterfront. I enjoyed the best seafood paella I have ever had. It was stewy and sprinkled liberally with prawns, squid, and other seafood goodies. Kibs turned to me and said,

"In case I forget, I want to say thank you for bringing me here."

I brushed off her thanks, just grateful that we were both enjoying ourselves.

After a perfect dinner, we headed back to the hotel on foot, realizing just how far we had walked all day. We walked along the waterfront, enjoying the palm trees and the tranquil breezes from the ocean. There were many people enjoying the area as well, from lovers cozying up to each other, to families celebrating birthdays. It was magical and peaceful.

The following morning, our driver showed up bright and early. We needed to leave before low tide or else there wouldn't be enough water for the boat. Our driver, Atílio, was pleasant but reserved. I was pleased to see that he was capable and confident as our lives were very much in his hands. He told us he was from Maputo and had practically been raised in the water. We headed towards Santa Maria beach first, avoiding exposed sandbars along the way. The blues and aquamarines of the shallow water near the sandbars were incredibly beautiful. We passed boats on the bars, fishermen in the water, and birds swooping low to catch a fish for breakfast.

Santa Maria beach was beautiful, peaceful and quiet. We were the only ones there when we showed up. Atílio brought snorkeling gear for us. We snorkeled for a couple hours in a sheltered part of the beach. Next, we headed to Inhaca Island for lunch, enjoying more acacia trees along the way. Lunch was more seafood. I had grilled crawfish and lobster, and thoroughly enjoyed it. After lunch, we headed to another beach on Portuguese Island. I walked the length of one side of the island while Kibs took a nap. Then I went for a swim to cool off. Kibs woke up and she was the most relaxed I had seen her since the trip began. We sat in the water and let the waves wash over us as we talked about life and possibilities. I thought to myself,

"It's moments like this that make life worth living."

Fluffy at Santa Maria beach

Alas, the wind picked up and Atílio determined that we would have trouble if we didn't leave a little early. He wasn't kidding. The ride back to Maputo was very bumpy, and my muscles remembered it for days afterwards.

We had a marvelous time and I still remember Mozambique fondly because of that day.

The next morning, it was cool and raining. I checked us out of the hotel while Kibs loaded the car. She came back in with a weird look on her face. Apparently, the mirror on our car had been stolen, although the thief kindly left the mirror holder behind. What followed was two hours of going back and forth with the hotel manager. He refused to admit fault even though we had been parked in the hotel parking spots our entire stay. There was always a security guard on duty so it's a mystery how the theft could have happened right in front of the hotel and the guard. We eventually convinced him to pay to have the mirror replaced.

One of the hotel employees took us deep into the city. There we found a man who cut out mirrors by hand. He traced the outline of our mirror holder, then cut out a piece of mirror that fit perfectly into our mirror holder. Based on our experience, I was sure he was kept very busy. The mirrors now had different magnification. It was really quite funny. But at least the new mirror was actually usable. Between the new mirror and the loud exhaust, which I was sure had a hole in it, I expected to pay severe fines when we returned the car. We left the hotel employee to pay and headed out of Maputo.

We got on the road to Johannesburg around 1 pm, three hours later than we had planned, but at least we now had a side mirror. We entered South Africa through the Ressano/Lebombo border. The holiday season was coming to an end so the border post was very busy with people returning home. As we waited in line on the South African side, we saw an army truck pull up with soldiers and Mozambican deportees in the back.

Nelson Mandela Bridge in Johannesburg

We left the border and drove to Joburg, stopping in Nelspruit for a late lunch. We finally got to Jozi around 8 pm. We spent the next day with Tavonga, a good friend of ours who lives in Jozi.

Everything I've ever heard about Joburg alludes to it being dangerous. For instance, I've heard that you can't stop at traffic lights or you'll be hijacked. So while I've flown through the airport a few times, I've never spent time in the city itself. Imagine my surprise when Tavonga took us around the city and it turned out to be hip and trendy. We were never bothered by anyone, even when we walked down the streets, taking pictures. It reinforced for me that you can't believe everything you're told about a place.

Joburg had the reputation for being dangerous especially in the '90s. Even though things have changed, the bad reputation remains.

Kibs and I were in an alright place and at first it looked like the trip would end on a good note. However, as soon as we got back to Joburg, her attitude changed and she became the same bitchy person she had been before the trip, being rude to people and insisting on getting her way. I asked Tavonga to take me dancing since this was my last night on the continent. He agreed right away, and asked for my preference of music. Kibs jumped in and insisted that Tavonga was too tired to take me dancing. She made such a fuss that in the end, I told Tavonga we would dance next time I was in town. At that point, I decided no matter what Kibs was going through, this was bitchy behavior. Our last night was spent in almost complete silence as I decided

"F*@# this sh*t."

and ignored her for the rest of the night. I focused on planning the next leg of my trip. When she left for her flight to Cape Town, she thanked me for the trip and told me how happy she was to have found herself. My expression called bullshit but I couldn't be bothered to actually say the words, as that would simply prolong the goodbye. After she left the hotel room, I danced a jig. I was that happy to be rid of her.

I was headed to the United Arab Emirates next. I was sad to leave my beloved continent, but excited about the next phase of the trip. I bade Africa a respectful farewell.

Tips for travel to Mozambique

- Ensure you have a blank page in your passport as the visa takes up a whole page.

- Beware of car mirror thieves. If you park at a hotel, check your car mirrors every day. If possible, scratch identifying marks or numbers into the mirror so it cannot be resold. That will deter thieves.

- Learn basic Portuguese.

- Choose your travel companions carefully. They can make or break your trip.

CHAPTER 5
ASIA

My 8 hour flight to the United Arab Emirates was direct from Johannesburg to Dubai. I prefer long flights because they give you a chance to settle in and really enjoy the trip. With short flights, you spend more time preparing for them than actually in the air.

My seat-mate was a South African oil and gas engineer who teaches in Saudi Arabia. We had a chat about the state of the oil and gas industry. One interesting thing I learned from him is that Cuba and Fidel Castro helped tremendously with the African countries' struggle for independence. He said Cuba is the only country to do so without colonizing them. I remembered that growing up in Zambia, I encountered many Cuban doctors who came over to the country as part of their training. I recall that Zambian doctors traveled to Cuba for their training as well.

My seatmate was really chatty but I was exhausted. As soon as it was polite to do so, I turned to my movies, eventually falling asleep.

FROM ANTARCTICA TO ZIMBABWE

United Arab Emirates

The Burj Al Arab Hotel in Dubai

It was nighttime when my flight arrived in Dubai. I was so excited to see this place I'd heard so much about. After getting through immigration, I caught a taxi. For the first time on my entire trip, my taxi driver was a woman. I was fascinated and really wanted to know how she became a taxi driver. Unfortunately, she spoke very little English so conversation was limited.

There were a lot of skyscrapers and they were all lit up. Dubai at night is very glittery and very sparkly. It reminded me of Las Vegas. My hotel was very grand and the service was impeccable. When I turned on the TV in my room, there was a personalized welcome waiting for me. I had the concierge book a tour of Dubai for the following day, and a tour of Abu Dhabi for the day after.

The UAE is made up of 7 Emirates: Dubai, Sharjah, Ajman, Ras al-Khaimah, Umm al-Quwain, Fujairah, and Abu

Dhabi which is the capital. Over 200 nationalities are represented in the UAE. In fact, over 80% of people in UAE are expatriates. During my entire trip, I never directly interacted with any Emiratis.

Skyline from the Dubai Marina

My driver on the tour of Dubai was from Pakistan. He worked full time in Dubai and visited his family once a year for 48 days. He was very pleasant and gave me an excellent tour of the city. I was blown away by the architecture. It wasn't just that there were a lot of skyscrapers; it was that they were all unique in some way. I imagined that Dubai would be a dream place for any architect.

We visited Za'abeel where Sheik Mohamed had his houses, offices and mosque. We went to Atlantis Hotel on the artificial archipelago of Palm Jumeirah. We visited the beautiful Burj Al Arab Hotel and Jumeriah beach. We stopped at the Dubai Marina and the Dubai Museum. Dubai was spectacular, albeit somewhat commercial.

That evening, I took a tour into the desert, and again my driver was from Pakistan. We went dune bashing, which is literally bashing the dunes with an SUV, and basically drifting on them. Later, we went to a desert camp where we rode camels for only about 2 minutes. The rest of the evening was food and entertainment in the form of belly dances and fire shows. It was winter so outside temperatures at night were around 60°F. Fortunately, I had my jacket with me. The experience was very commercialized and felt somewhat cheap. Overall, it was less impressive than my desert experience in the Sahara, or even in the Namib. But the sand in the lungs at the end of it was the same. I had a cough for the next two or three days.

All day I couldn't get Kibs out of my mind. I had finally transcended from feeling sorry for her to being furious with her. It became clear to me that she had done a lot maliciously to try to sabotage my trip, even though I was trying to help her. I hated that I was still allowing her to ruin my trip.

I decided to send her a text detailing how I felt, my disappointment and my anger. As I wrote, the text grew longer and longer until it became more like a letter. But I was able to get all my feelings out. As soon as I sent it, I felt a million times better. I asked her to either apologize without making excuses, or not to bother responding. She apologized. It was one of those weak apologies:

> "I'm sorry if I've ever hurt you,"

without her actually acknowledging any of the things she did. I decided she wasn't worth any more of my attention.

This experience was tough for me as it essentially ended in the death of a lifelong friendship. I understand that stress can change people but that doesn't excuse bad behavior. My own part in it was that I allowed her to behave this way. If I could do it over, I would have cut her loose after Namibia, or after Durban. The experience really taught me that I am much too patient with people.

In 2014, my motto for the year was

"YOLO,"

i.e. You Only Live Once; in 2015, it was

"No Ragrets,"

spelled wrongly to emphasize that one should regret nothing. I decided that my 2016 motto would be

"F*@# this sh*t."

to remind me to end bad situations before they get out of hand. No more burning myself to keep other people warm.

I put Kibs out of my mind and I was able to really enjoy the rest of my trip. Now I only bring her up to illustrate that you can't trust everyone. It took some time but I did realize eventually that jealousy explains her behavior better than stress. She was jealous of me, which blows my mind. I recall catching her giving me funny looks from time to time. When I remembered those looks, it finally clicked that she was jealous of me. She envied that I had a carefree attitude even though I was jobless with no idea of what the future held for me. She hated the fact that I was living my dream and traveling the world. She was jealous of the fact that I spent money easily, whenever I wanted or needed to. I couldn't have imagined that this person, who was a sister that I chose, not one I was born with, would ever be jealous of me. After all, I included her on part of my trip and would have helped her in any way I could.

Like I said, it was a huge learning experience. Now I am more cautious about sharing things with people. And I am much quicker to nip things in the bud, if they are not going how they should. In other words,

"F*@# this sh*t."

The following day, I was picked up from my hotel for my tour of Abu Dhabi. My driver was Pakistani again, and my companions were Italian and French. I discussed my trip with them and the Italians recommended that I go to Macau when I got to Hong Kong.

Abu Dhabi is about an hour and a half from Dubai. Our first stop was Ferrari World which is a Ferrari-branded indoor amusement park. We didn't ride any rides but we got to wander around and admire the Ferraris that were on display. We stopped at the Emirates Palace Hotel, which was dripping with opulence. The expensive cars in front attested to the wealth of the hotel's clientele. We spent some time at the Sheikh Zayed Mosque. My guide provided me with appropriate covering, a long dress or abaya, and a headscarf. These are also provided free of charge at the mosque. The mosque was beautiful, made with materials from all around the world. The exterior has 82 white domes which contrasted strikingly with the blue sky. The pillars, stained glass and finery make this mosque too elegant for words.

The architecture in Abu Dhabi was just as interesting and unique as Dubai's. Abu Dhabi appeared to be a little quieter and less glitzy.

In front of Sheikh Zayed Mosque

We stopped for lunch at the Marina Mall. After lunch, my companions and I tried to find the restrooms. The women's restroom was not far from the food court. Unlike everywhere else I've ever been, the men's restroom was nowhere close by. We eventually found it clear across the other side of the mall. I walked into the women's restroom and I saw the saddest looking cleaning lady I have ever seen. She was a young Chinese woman, in her late twenties. She looked like she had just received devastating news. She sat cross-legged on a counter with her head bowed and tears streaming down her face while she looked at her phone. I wanted to help so badly but I didn't know what to say or how. I left her alone but I wish I had at least said something to her, just so she knew someone cared that she was sad.

After lunch, we went to the Heritage Village which is a recreated traditional village. One can see a traditional tent, craftsmen at work, and other aspects of traditional life. That was the last stop on our tour. I left my group and had dinner with a classmate from high school and his wife. They have lived and worked in Abu Dhabi for years so they offered much insight into the country. I explained that I was having a hard time getting a feel for the culture especially since everyone I met there was also a foreigner. They recommended avoiding Dubai and Abu Dhabi, and going to another of the Emirates, like Sharjah. There things are apparently closer to the old culture.

My next destination was Thailand. I boarded the plane the next morning and headed for Bangkok, one of my favorite cities in the world.

Tips for travel to the United Arab Emirates

- Visit in winter when temperatures are bearable.

- Dress modestly.

- Public displays of affection are not allowed.

- To experience local culture, visit Sharjah or other Emirates besides Dubai and Abu Dhabi.

DR. QUINTA

Thailand

Fluffy and I in front of a Buddhist Shrine

The flight to Bangkok was uneventful. I had visited Bangkok just eight months prior and had enjoyed the sights, the food, the shopping. I was back so that I could spend quality time with Api, my best friend from graduate school who lived there.

As my cab drove away from Suvarnabhumi Airport, the driver covered the meter and asked me to pay a flat fee instead. I was aware of this popular scam so I declined and asked him to take me back to the airport. When we got back, I made sure to report him. I got another cab and this time there were no issues.

I had picked a hotel close to the MBK shopping center. One of my favorite activities in Bangkok is shopping. There are so many clothes and shoe malls that I wasn't able to get to half of them on my last visit. The clothes fit me perfectly and cost very little. I wanted to be close to the malls this time. My suitcase did not have much extra room but I was getting to the end of my trip. I was sure I could find room for a couple new items.

Mango dessert, pomelo salad, and noodle soup

Api and I had street food for dinner. Nothing beats having some form of noodle soup late at night on the streets of Bangkok. Afterwards, we had my favorite dessert in Bangkok: mango ice cream with mango sticky rice, with slices of actual mango. Thai food is among the best food in the world, in my opinion. The night markets run from 5 pm to 3 or 4 in the morning so the streets are always very lively. I love that Bangkok never sleeps.

There is a lot to do in Bangkok: you can visit temples like the Grand Palace and Wat Pho which is the Temple of the Reclining Buddha; visit the floating market; attend a muay thai tournament; eat lots of cheap and delicious fruit and food; and, of course, shop. You can also get a suit custom made in only a few days and for a really good price.

If you have time, there is even more to do outside of Bangkok: the tiger temple where you can pose with the tigers, white water rafting, riding elephants, etc. Having already done most of these things, I decided to take it easy and just enjoy Api's company. We ate a lot, then we shopped a lot, then we ate some more.

Thai people are very hospitable and tourists are treated very well. However, be on the lookout for scams. Cab drivers may try to overcharge you. Always insist on them using the meter. At the temples, you may be told that the temple is temporarily closed to non-Thai people and they will try to take you to places where they will try to sell you a tour, clothing or jewelry. Ignore them.

I knew that my trip around the world was coming to an end. I had been very disciplined and had refrained from buying clothes I didn't need. But as soon as I got to Bangkok, I knew I couldn't hold back any longer. Most clothes sold in Thailand are size 3, which fits me perfectly. Most times, you are not allowed to try clothes on before you buy them. I became skilled at assessing whether clothes would fit me. I bought a few clothes and a couple pairs of shoes. Somehow, I managed to get everything into my suitcase.

I decided to visit other countries in the region. Fortunately, there are several budget airlines which made traveling around Asia very affordable. I decided to go to Hong Kong next. I booked my flight and hotel, bade Api farewell, and headed to Hong Kong.

Tips for travel to Thailand

- Pack an adaptor for electrical outlets.

- Hold on to immigration card from the airport. You will need it to leave the country.

- Watch out for scams. You may be told that temples are restricted to only Thai people at certain times. This is not true.

- If you take a taxi, insist on the driver using the meter.

Hong Kong

Hong Kong buses

I arrived in Hong Kong and went through immigration with no issues. Once outside, I grabbed a cab and headed to my hotel on Hong Kong Island. To my dismay, it was chilly and raining when I arrived. My hotel room was well appointed although on the small side, like the hotels in Europe. I loved the window seat in my room and I spent many hours sitting there and looking out at the city.

Thanks to Yelp, I was able to find restaurants near my hotel. I had been informed by many that food in Hong Kong is amazing. So, of course, I tried different types of food while I was there. They were all awful. They tasted different from anything I've ever had before, but not in a good way. I'm sure the places I tried were authentic because they were packed with Chinese people. They spoke no English although they did have an English menu. I found out later that prices are inflated on the English menus.

The first dish I tried was rice with scrambled egg and shrimp. It was revolting. The egg was only partly scrambled leading to the slimiest meal I've ever eaten. It was flavorless and horrible and I couldn't finish it. Because I was still hungry, I found a pub and ordered a fish burger with fries cooked in duck fat. While I waited, I was regaled by very loud '90s gangster rap. When the food came, it was delicious and I hungrily gobbled it all up.

The next day, I tried another Chinese place. It was packed with locals so I knew this was the real deal. I had shrimp in rice paper and a giant dumpling with some kind of meat. The shrimp wasn't terrible but the dumpling tasted disgusting. I sat next to a nice girl from Hong Kong who told me what sauces to add to the dumpling. The sauces made no difference, except to make the dumpling taste worse. As before, I could not finish the meal. I left and found a nice tea house near my hotel. I ordered pancakes, which I normally wouldn't eat, and tea.

Because it rained the whole time I was in Hong King, I decided my best bet to see the whole island would be to take a sightseeing bus. I waited for more than 30 minutes at the stop, in the cold and rain. The bus never showed up even though it is supposed to run at 20 minute intervals. I was cold and miserable so I gave up.

"F*@# this sh*t."

I left the bus stop and returned to my hotel.

Overall, my stay in Hong Kong was disappointing. The main attraction for me was the food, and that didn't work out so well. It did, however, help me understand why the Chinese tourists on my cruise to Antarctica had brought their own food along. I now understand how different their cuisine is, and I was more sympathetic to them.

I would re-visit Hong Kong, but I would wait for the summer. I would also get specific recommendations on good restaurants to try. My companions in Abu Dhabi had recommended visiting Macau, so I may do that next time.

My next destination was Singapore. I made my travel arrangements, then sat on the window seat of my hotel room, enjoying the view of the mountains peeking through the fog.

Tips for travel to Hong Kong

- Hold on to immigration card. You will need it to leave the country.

- Dress warmly in the winter (December to February).

- If you can't stomach local Chinese food, you can find every other kind of cuisine very easily.

- Yelp is a good resource for finding restaurants in Hong Kong.

Singapore

Gardens by the Bay showing domes and supertrees

I was happy to head south to Singapore, where it was much warmer. My flight had left Hong Kong so early that most shops were not yet open, so I couldn't buy any souvenirs. I made sure I bought refrigerator magnets upon my arrival in Singapore. One of the magnets had some interesting Singaporean laws printed on it: no chewing gum, no spitting, no smoking, no littering, no vandalism, and no using the toilet without flushing. It also listed the fines associated with breaking each rule. Luckily for me, I had run out of chewing gum in Thailand. Singapore Changi Airport was beautiful with many live plants and mini gardens.

I was still dealing with a slight cough from going into the Arabian Desert. It felt like there was a tiny drop of liquid floating in the back of my throat, and no matter how hard I coughed, it wouldn't be dislodged. Sadly, I had left my sister's medicine in Johannesburg to create space for other things. The chilly Hong Kong air hadn't helped but I was hoping warm weather would. It was bright and sunny as my cab drove me to my hotel. Then it started to rain. I was disappointed. I only had one day to spend in Singapore and the rain could possibly prevent me from enjoying the city.

After I checked in, I went to the bus stop just outside my hotel and caught a sightseeing bus. I enjoyed seeing the different parts of Singapore despite the pouring rain. A friend had recommended the Gardens by the Bay so I got off there. The stop is right outside the Boat Building, so I took a few minutes to walk through this marvelous hotel building. Fortunately for me, the rain stopped just then. I walked to the Gardens by the Bay, enjoying the greenery, and the flowers, and the view of the gardens.

The Boat Building

I decided to check out the Future of Us Exhibition before going to the gardens. It basically went over the history of the country and talked about developments especially in technology that the country was going into. A powerful quite from the exhibition was,

> "The future is not set, just as the past was not."

For some reason, that quote stayed with me. It triggered a great depth of self-reflection for me, the likes of which I had not done since I left Morocco. In one of the halls, I got a chance to see dreams that others had submitted and I got a chance to submit my own:

> "I want to change the world. I want the world to be different because I was here."

I actually got teary-eyed, realizing that I do want to make a difference in this world.

I left the exhibition and walked to the gardens. I started by taking a closer look at some of the supertrees. The supertrees are tall structures that look like trees with heights up to 160 feet. As I got closer to them, I realized they actually have real plants incorporated into them. They looked like something out of a science fiction movie.

I headed again towards the Gardens by the Bay. The gardens are essentially greenhouses, and each has a specific type of climate. I visited the Flower Dome first. It was blazing hot outside by this time so the shade inside was very welcome. The Flower Dome features a Mediterranean-type climate, i.e. summer drought. It was spectacular. As soon as I walked in, I was captivated by the flowers, the cacti, the greenery, and the plant sculptures. It was huge, and covered about 3 acres. Although packed with tourists, it was still such a tranquil environment that I spent hours in there. I visited the Cloud Forest next and it was almost as riveting. It was a tropical mountain environment with a cooling waterfall falling down a mountain. I rode the elevator to the "lost world" enjoying the incredible views and beautiful plants. I had many random people come up to me to take pictures. I humored all of them, pretending I was some famous person traveling incognito.

There are other parts to the Gardens by the Bay, but I only had time for these two. I kept in mind that the sightseeing buses stopped running around 5:30 pm, so I forced myself to leave at around 5 pm. I caught the sightseeing bus again and saw other sights in Singapore, and was finally dropped off at my hotel. I realized I hadn't eaten a full meal all day. I found a restaurant close by, and had delicious dim sum for dinner.

Monkey sculptures in the Flower Dome

Overall, I enjoyed Singapore and would certainly return. The most impressive part for me was how the citizens are included in planning the future of the country. The Future of Us Exhibition really made an impression on me. The people were pleasant, and I never had any issues dealing with them. Singapore reminded me of Rwanda, in a way. They have a similar history in that an authoritarian government sped up the development of both countries. Both have rules in place that make them attractive to international investors. The results of that are obvious in Singapore's prosperity and wealth. Rwanda is well on its way to being similarly successful.

The next morning, I left for Kuala Lumpur, Malaysia. At the airport, I was impressed to see that the terminals were divided by region you were flying to, e.g. South East Asia, Africa, etc. I thought about what it would be like to live in Singapore. The cost of buying and owning a car is purposely prohibitive, but there is plenty of efficient public transportation. I could see myself living there, at least for a few years. I needed to figure out how to convince Hubby it would be a good move.

Tips for travel to Singapore

- Do not pack any chewing gum. Do not chew gum in public. You will be fined.

- Do not enter the country with cigarettes or you may be fined.

- Hold on to immigration card. You will need it to leave the country.

- English is widely spoken in Singapore.

Malaysia

Petronas Towers

I went through immigration in Kuala Lumpur with no issues. I took a cab to my hotel which was very close to the Petronas Towers, the iconic symbols of the city. Jerry, one of my best friends from graduate school, is from Malaysia. He was not in the country at the time but he arranged for his brother, Morgan, to pick me up from Kuala Lumpur International Airport and show me around the city.

When I got off the plane, I went to the area where Morgan had asked me to meet him. I realized it was only cabs. I waited around but did not see Morgan. I could not get the airport Wi-Fi at that location so I could not call him. I debated with myself, trying to decide what to do. I only had twenty four hours in Malaysia and I felt like I was wasting that time. After twenty minutes, I decided

"F*@# this sh*t."

I caught a cab to my hotel and called Morgan from there. He had shown up at the airport but obviously couldn't find me. He was still willing to take me around the city. He picked me up from the hotel and the sight-seeing/food-eating began.

Malaysian food

Our first stop was Chinatown. Jerry FaceTimed us from the US to give his brother instructions on where to take me and what kind of food to get me. He was right on every count. We moved from restaurants to stalls, picking up different delicious food items. We got caught in a downpour so we stopped to grab dessert until the rain let up.

Later, we walked to a nearby Buddhist temple. It's always uncomfortable for me taking pictures in temples while people are praying. I always feel like I'm being disrespectful. We stayed for about 10 minutes then left. I was stuffed to the gills so we took a break on the eating until dinner.

In the meantime, I went shopping at Sungei Wang mall. The mall was a good place to shop for clothes but was even better than Bangkok for shoes. I found myself buying a few pairs, knowing that I had no space in my luggage. I returned to my hotel with my new shoes and rested for a few minutes before I was picked up for dinner. We had dinner at a lovely restaurant at Suria Mall. The durian-based dessert was the highlight of the evening for me.

The next morning, I checked out and Morgan took me to the airport. On the way, we stopped and had roti for breakfast at a mama stall at Jerry's recommendation. He also recommended tea with milk and sugar, which I love. I loved everything he recommended. I am really glad to have such a great friend. He was an excellent host, despite the fact that he wasn't even in the country. The generosity and hospitality of his brother and his family was much appreciated.

After I arrived at the airport, I checked in for my flight on Malaysia Airlines. Knowing their recent history with losing a plane full of passengers, I knew I was being extremely brave to fly with them. But they had the only flights that let me sleep until a reasonable time and still arrive in Bangkok with plenty of time for my flight to Sydney, Australia.

There was slight turbulence during the flight, and to my amusement, everyone on board let out a scream, myself included. Still, we arrived in Bangkok in one piece. To my annoyance, I had to go through immigration to be able to get on my Sydney flight. Fortunately, I had plenty of extra time. I bought mangoes and guavas to munch on while I waited for boarding. My new shoes were in a shopping bag. They wouldn't fit into my suitcase so I caved and bought a small duffel bag.

I couldn't believe I had made it to all 4 countries on such a tight schedule. I was mentally and physically exhausted, and couldn't wait to get on the plane so I could sit back and relax for the 9+ hours the flight would take.

Tips for travel to Malaysia

- Pack light clothing to help deal with the heat and humidity.

- Although credit cards are accepted at malls and restaurants, you will need cash for many smaller vendors.

- Budget airlines such as Air Asia make travel around Asia really cheap. Consider flying to move more quickly from one part of Malaysia to another.

- Show up ready to eat.

CHAPTER 6
OCEANIA

On the plane to Sydney, I decided it was a good time to write down my New Year's resolutions. I came up with the following list:

- Read at least one book a month
- Improve my Spanish
- Improve my piano skills
- Learn how to play the guitar
- Start my own company
- Apply for a job at NASA
- Get a literary agent / Publish a book
- Take up salsa dancing
- Take up kickboxing

They all seemed doable and achievable. Besides, if I didn't push myself beyond my self-imposed limits, I wouldn't be able to achieve the things that I have only been able to imagine.

Australia

Sydney Opera House

My arrival in Sydney was less than pleasant. After going through immigration, I waited at baggage claim for my bag. As I waited, I was approached by a security agent who had a lot of questions for me. Was I traveling alone? Did I only have one bag? Where was I coming from? How long was the flight? Where was I going next? When she started asking questions I had already answered, I had to ask her if there was a problem. She replied no and moved off to harass someone else. Intellectually, I knew that I probably fit the description of a drug mule as seen on *Locked Up Abroad*:

- Little or no luggage
- I was flying to a different place than where I arrived from
- I was only staying for 2 days

Still, it gave me a bad first impression, and that impression still clouds my memories of Australia.

It is forbidden to bring live plants or animals, or certain products derived from them into Australia. This is to prevent the unique flora and fauna of Australia from contamination from the outside world.

As usual, I took a cab to my hotel. Still exhausted from my trip through Asia, I decided to clean up and get some sleep in my smallish hotel room. That evening, I forced myself to get up and I had dinner at a nearby restaurant.

The following day was sunny and bright. With renewed vigor, I hit the streets. I was staying close to the harbor so I headed in that direction. I walked for a while with an older gentleman who worked in the mining industry. I could tell he was seriously hitting on me. He made sure I ended up at the right place, gave me his phone number, then went on his way.

I walked around the harbor, enjoying the hustle and bustle of people around me. There were many restaurants and shops. I saw a few entertainers making money from tourists' tips. I sat down with two Aborigines, playing the clapsticks while one of them played the didjeridoo.

I made it a point to go to the Sydney Opera House, which was quite impressive in person. After I took enough pictures of the opera house and the Sydney Harbor Bridge, I caught a sightseeing bus, and learned quite a bit about the history of Sydney. I returned at the end of the tour, and found a nice restaurant with outdoor seating. It was nice watching people go by as I enjoyed my meal. I could have sat there all day.

I was impressed by the unique but professional business

clothes worn by the people in the neighborhood of my hotel. My waitress directed me to some nearby malls. To my dismay, it started raining before I made it there and I was forced to stop and buy an umbrella. I saw three people trip on my way to the mall: a construction worker, a girl on a curb, and a man who slipped in the middle of the street and landed on his bum. I'm not sure if it was coincidence or if Australians are clumsier than the rest of us. I treaded carefully so I wouldn't fall as well. I found the mall and bought some very well made business dresses. I made my way back to my hotel through the rain.

Playing the clapsticks with an Aborigine

I checked out of my hotel the next day, this time heading for French Polynesia. Hubby would be joining me in Tahiti. It had been three months since I left the US. I couldn't wait to see him. I had been keeping him abreast of my activities and location every day. I usually downplayed the bad incidents like Kibs' bad behavior, while making the fun events sound even more interesting. I really didn't want him to worry unless there was a good reason.

Tips for travel to Australia

- Do not bring any live plants or animals into Australia. Some plant and animal products will not be allowed through Customs.

- Credit cards are widely accepted.

- Tour buses are a great way to explore Sydney.

- Australia is quite expensive. Prepare to spend a lot of money.

French Polynesia

Hotel on the island of Bora Bora

I flew from Sydney to Tahiti via Auckland. Upon arrival in Pape'ete, Tahiti, myself and the other passengers were welcomed by a singing duo and a dancing lady dressed in traditional Polynesian attire. I started to get into holiday mode. French Polynesia was my gift to myself. I planned to relax and not worry about doing activities or seeing any sites in particular. I would just let things happen here.

I crossed the International Date Line (IDL) when I flew from Auckland to Pape'ete. That had some serious implications. We had made reservations at a hotel near Faa'a International Airport. It turned out that the bookings had been made for a day later. Essentially, I went back in time by 24 hours when I crossed the IDL, so I had no hotel reservation when I arrived. Fortunately, there were vacancies available so I canceled the old reservation and made a new one. Several other guests trying to check in found out they had made the same error so that made me feel better. Our flight to Bora Bora was leaving the following day, not that day as I had thought. I hoped all our other reservations were correct.

I had no way to communicate with Hubby since his flight was still in the air, or so I hoped. I arrived at approximately 1 am. I left word with the front desk that I was expecting him and went to sleep. I kept getting woken up by text messages on WhatsApp. I didn't want to silence my phone in case Hubby sent a message. So I drifted in and out of sleep. Finally, around 5 am, the front desk called and said he was coming up.

I was so pleased to see him, this husband of mine who had made this trip happen for me. We exchanged travel stories then went to breakfast. Afterwards, we tried to go to sleep. We were awoken by the hotel calling to see if we were checking out. Hubby went down to sort out the reservations. While he was gone, I fell asleep but was awoken by staff knocking on the door, then entering the room to clean. I pretty much gave up on sleeping after that. We took showers then went for a walk around the area, eventually grabbing an early dinner. The mosquitoes were very into us and we had to buy insect repellent.

The next morning, we took a cab to the airport to catch a flight to Bora Bora. Our driver was eccentric to say the least. At a stop while waiting for cross traffic, she pulled out a ukulele and started playing and singing. She also gave me a flower for my hair to show that I was taken as per Polynesian tradition. Then she gave me another for the other side of my hair, to confuse people into thinking I was available. She was a hoot.

We flew on a tiny plane from Pape'ete to Bora Bora. Next we took a fifteen minute boat ride on a boat sent by our hotel. The service at the hotel was excellent. After our butler gave us a tour of the resort, he took us to our suite which was over the water. There was champagne and chocolates waiting for us. Our suite was easily 2,000 square foot with a separate bedroom, bathroom, and living room. We could see the water through glass in the floor of the bathroom and living room. We had a deck with cushioned deck chairs on it. Stairs led off the side of the deck into the water. The water was the bluest I have ever seen anywhere, rivaled only by the Caribbean. The beauty of it was breathtaking. This was the end of my trip and I fully intended to relax and enjoy myself.

View while snorkeling

We learned that *iorana* means hello, and *maruuru* means thank you. Beyond that, it was difficult to get to know Polynesian culture. French culture was easy to find, but that wasn't what I was hoping for. I did learn that Polynesians have the most amazing tattoos, and they often have deep meanings. The tattoos are structured yet flowy. The influence of the ocean is obvious. My favorite waiter had a tattoo on his arm to commemorate his relationship with his late father.

Bora Bora

There were many activities at the resort. We could kayak, paddle board, swim, work out, snorkel, etc. There was a game room where we could play pool, read, or surf the web on hotel computers. We could, of course, watch TV in our suite, if we wanted to. Bicycles were provided so we could get from one end of the resort to another quickly. Golf carts and drivers were available if we were patient enough to call for them and wait.

We had absolutely no agenda and it was great. On each of the five days we spent on Bora Bora, we woke up and did whatever we felt like doing on that day. Some days, we left the curtains open in our room so we could watch the sun rise over the ocean. The ninja mosquitoes were present here in Bora Bora too, so I skipped sunscreen in favor of insect repellent. The water was also the saltiest I've ever tasted. But these were minor things and didn't distract from the beauty around us.

My favorite activity was snorkeling. We spent many hours enjoying the schools of fish swimming around coral. It was so peaceful and time slipped by without us realizing it.

The most memorable day, however, was the day I refer to as "The Curse of the Black Pearl." No, I did not see Captain Jack Sparrow but I did catch a glimpse of Davy Jones' locker. I'll preface this by saying French Polynesia is well known for its black pearls. They were available for sale at the resort. When we woke up on that fateful day, Hubby remarked on how strong the wind was. He was right. The cushions on our deck chairs were being blown off. Still, we went paddle boarding, and like an idiot, I didn't wear a life jacket. My intention was to paddle close to shore but the current was so strong that day that I found myself much further out than I wanted. In a flash, I teetered and fell off the board and I heard Hubby fall off his board too. The first sensation was the stinging of salt water in my eyes and I had to shut my eyes from the pain. My expensive sunglasses fell off and with one eye open and full of salt water, I watched them sink gently to the bottom of the Pacific Ocean.

Now, I am not the strongest swimmer but I *can* swim and I can easily float on my back. I held on to the paddle and tried to make my way to the board. It kept getting further and further away from me thanks to the strong current. Eventually, I dropped the paddle and struck out for the board. I couldn't catch up to it. I started to tire. I ran through the possibilities in my mind. I knew Hubby could save me but last time I had eyes on him, he was in front of me and heading away from me. I didn't know if he knew I had fallen. I looked to shore. There were people sunning themselves on the beach but they looked so far away. I was sure they couldn't reach me in time. Thinking back, I could have swum back to shore but in my panicked state, I couldn't think straight. I figured my best bet was Hubby coming back for me. I yelled his name with all my strength. I kept shouting for him while trying to stay afloat. It never occurred to me to float on my back or swim to him. I was panicking too much.

Polynesian dancers

I was probably only in the water for a couple minutes but it felt like a lifetime. The sight of Hubby paddling towards me is the most welcome sight of my life to date. I swam towards him, casually as he remembers it, and held on to his board. The poor guy was panting with all the effort it had taken for him to head back to me. My favorite waiter had heard me from the shore and made it to me a few seconds after Hubby did. I will never forget his face either. For the rest of the day, I wore a life vest no matter what we were doing. I bought a black pearl that day, to sort of commemorate not drowning in paradise.

On our last evening, we were treated to Polynesian dances and songs. The entertainers invited some of the guests to join them. I was one of the lucky chosen ones. They taught us some of the dances and we had to entertain the other guests. It was all great fun.

The next day, we packed our bags sadly. Fortunately, it was chilly and raining. It made us less sad to be leaving this paradise.

We flew back to Pape'ete. I was leaving for Los Angeles that evening while Hubby was flying out the following morning. We checked into a hotel, then took a cab to downtown Pape'ete. We walked around the city, noting that there was a pearl shop on almost every block. We found some beautiful carved black pearls, and I bought some to add to my collection. They represent a new chance at life for me.

We walked into a random restaurant and had the most delicious meal. It was a dish of black beans with green vegetables, macaroni, and pork called *ma'a ti nto*. I was excited at finding some authentic Polynesian food until the restaurant owner told me it was actually Chinese food. It was good, wherever it came from.

Hubby riding off into the sunset

I boarded my flight later that evening and headed to Los Angeles. I was both happy and sad that my trip was coming to an end.

Tips for travel to French Polynesia

- You will most likely be crossing the International Date Line. Double check arrival dates and times.

- Brush up on your French.

- Bora Bora is expensive. Prepare your mind and wallet for the cost in advance, so you can relax and enjoy yourself when you get there.

- Book plane shuttles early as they travel between islands only once a day.

CHAPTER 7
NORTH AMERICA

The last log of my trip was North America. I was ending up where I had started. I was heading to Los Angeles first, then Hubby and I would head to Trinidad for Carnival. I love long flights. It annoys me to spend hours preparing for a flight only to spend 2 hours in the air. An 8 hour flight such as this allowed me to truly relax. I watched shows on my iPad, read a book, slept and ate. It was a good flight.

As we approached L.A., I apprehensively waited for the air hostesses to collect the blankets. This is such a heartless practice carried out by many airlines. It leaves passengers cold and uncomfortable for the last 45 minutes of the flight. I was pleased that Air Tahiti did not do that.

It was with both joy and sorrow that I set foot again on US soil.

U.S.A

Hollywood

The plane landed in Los Angeles, and for the first time in three months, I was able to take my phone off airplane mode. Text messages and voicemails poured in. I ignored them all and went straight to Reddit. Thanks to Global Entry, going through immigration was a breeze and I was done in five minutes.

It felt bittersweet to be back. I thought back on all the adventures I'd been through. Life had been so exciting for the last three months. I never knew what each day was going to bring. Going back home meant everything would be predictable, and inevitably, boring.

I was flying from L.A. to Houston but I had an 8 hour layover. Since it was my first time in L.A., I decided to leave the airport and explore the city. After checking my bags, I took a bus to Hollywood for only $8. I caught a sightseeing bus and took a tour of Hollywood and Beverly Hills. It was weird and very commercial. A lot of the sights were along the lines of: here is the club where this comedian first played, or this is the motel where this movie star overdosed.

I got bored and got off the bus at the La Brea Tar Pits. They are a collection of pits where heavy crude oil has seeped to the surface. In the past, animals would get stuck in them and their bones would be preserved. Nowadays, the pits are fenced off to keep people and animals from stepping on them. A lot of excavation of bones from as far back as 38,000 years is going on today. I learned that L.A. was an oil boom town and a lot of oil is still produced in L.A. County.

Fluffy in Hollywood

I caught another sightseeing tour bus, finished the rest of the tour, and then returned to the airport. I boarded my flight to Houston where Hubby and I spent a few days. Then we packed our bags and headed to Trinidad for Carnival.

Tips for travel to the US

- Ensure you have at least 4 hours between flights if initial landing in US is not final destination. Going through immigration and security can take a long time.

- Credit cards are accepted almost everywhere.

- Although the country is well-connected by roads, it is vast. Flying from one area to another may be better than driving everywhere, if time is a concern.

- Get Global Entry if you can. It will save you plenty of time when you re-enter the US. It also gives TSA PreCheck privileges for local flights.

Trinidad

Carnival in Port of Spain

Hubby and I boarded the plane to Port of Spain, Trinidad. Our flight was five hours long and direct to Port of Spain. There were no movies offered, and no food except for a small bag of peanuts. I sighed. I'd been spoiled traveling in other countries. Most airlines still feed you a whole meal, even if you are only traveling for a couple hours, but not US-based airlines.

When we arrived in Port of Spain, the line at immigration was hours long. Clearly, there were a lot of people showing up for Carnival. We stayed with the family of a friend as hotels were sold out.

So our friend was not able to travel to Trinidad with us but his mother Moira was more than happy to have Hubby and I stay with her. It was a little awkward as we had never met before but it was better than paying $1,000 a night for a hotel.

It was after 9 pm when we emerged from Piarco International Airport. Moira and her sister were waiting to give us a ride to Moira's house. We had plans to attend a party that night and we picked their brains for how we would get to the party. As it turned out, taxis are really hard to come by during Carnival. Moira said she would drop us off at the party. She was kind enough to make us a light dinner, although we begged her not to. We didn't want to inconvenience her.

As we settled in, Moira warned us that her area of town was having issues with water pressure. She said,

"If you open the tap and no water comes out, just wait five minutes and try again."

That seemed like an easy fix. I went to go wash my hands and sure enough, no water came out of the tap. I waited five minutes and tried again. There was still no water. I figured "five minutes" was a euphemism for a little while. I decided I would try again later.

After we ate, I needed to pee. The toilet would not flush, and the taps had no water so I couldn't wash my hands. I started to worry.

Moira drove us to the party. It was more like an outdoor concert. There were hundreds of people and lots of food and booze. Because of barriers, Moira could not drive close enough to the site. She parked the car, then walked us to exactly where we needed to be. She actually held my hand too. I felt like an idiot as we passed plenty of party-goers who stared at us, wondering what the heck was happening. It felt like my own mother was holding my hand to make sure I didn't try to escape. It was humiliating at the time but kind of funny now.

We met with friends at the concert and we had a great time. I saw the artists dabbing and I could not understand what they were doing. I had been out of the loop while traveling and I assumed it was a Caribbean thing. It was days later that I expressed my confusion and Hubby explained the whole phenomenon to me. I still think it's strange.

We shared a taxi ride with our friends to get home the next morning. It was just after 7 am when we arrived at Moira's. She was up, and had just finished cooking lunch for us. She was heading out to a meeting and wouldn't be back till late afternoon. Again, we felt bad that she was going to so much trouble on our behalf.

We were exhausted from a whole night of partying. I wanted to take a shower before going to bed. I turned on the shower but no water came out. I waited five, then ten, then fifteen minutes. Still no water. I was starting to get frustrated. I looked around for containers of water. I have visited quite a few places where water shortages are common. The people I stayed with in those places would always have several drums and buckets filled with water. There was not a single container of water in Moira's house.

Unfortunately for us, she had left already. I really wanted to know how she got ready that morning with no water available. Did she have a stash she was hiding from us? Frustrated, I went to bed, dirty and sweaty.

We slept until 3 in the afternoon. We reasoned the water had to be on by now. Hubby left for the restroom. He returned ten seconds later, and I will never forget the look on his face. The look of a man who needs to poop but can't because there is no water. I decided then

"F*@# this sh*t."

We would pay $1,000 a night if that was what we had to do, but I was getting my husband somewhere where he could poop in peace.

I started searching online for hotels with vacancies. I got really lucky, and found that the Hyatt Regency had a room available. I was over the moon. Even the $500 a night price tag didn't faze me. I needed water at any cost. I booked the room, then called the Hyatt to make sure they had water. I could almost hear the quizzical expression of the woman on the other end of the phone as she said,

"Yes, of *course*, ma'am, we have water."

We were ecstatic. We got dressed and packed our things immediately. We left a note for Moira on her dining table. We called her for good measure with the phone she had loaned us but she didn't pick up. To be sure we covered all our bases, we called her son and explained the situation to him. Then we sent her a text on WhatsApp. That's how guilty we felt about leaving but nothing would make me stay a moment more than I needed to.

Fortunately for us, we always travel light. We both had a backpack and a small suitcase. We walked down to the main street to try to hail a cab. Of course, Hubby stepped in dog poop on the way, which was insulting, cause I know he was holding in his own poop.

We tried hailing a cab for a couple hours but there were no cabs. The buses that passed by were all going the opposite direction to where we needed to go. At around the two hour mark, we saw Moira get off a minibus and walk to her house. I don't know if she saw us but she never looked in our direction.

Shortly after that, an unlicensed cab stopped for us. He quoted us a price and because of the Nigerian in me, I haggled to bring it down even though we were desperate. After we agreed on a price, we put our luggage in the trunk and headed to the Hyatt.

When we arrived at the Hyatt, I swear I saw the clouds open up and angels singing. Outside the hotel were people dressed up in costume welcoming guests. We were given champagne to sip on while we went through the registration process. They also gave us t-shirts and goodie bags with useful items for Carnival like sunscreen. The best part was that the hotel provided a free shuttle for the guests to any part of the island. The hotel was near the parade route and the concierge kept track of where the Carnival was at all times so she could direct guests to the right location.

As soon as we got to our room, Hubby took a much needed poop, and I took the longest, hottest shower I had in a long time.

There were many parties in the days leading to Carnival. Trinidadians can party like no other nationalities I've met. Partying until morning for a week straight seemed quite normal for them. We held on for as long as we could then took a break to gather our strength before the first parade started. We picked up our costumes two days before the first parade.

Bake n' shark

The first parade went from morning to night but most people only wore part of their costume. Even then, I felt overdressed in my shorts. On the actual day of Carnival, or *playing mas* as they say in Trinidad, everyone was fully decked out. Makeup and glitter, skimpy outfits, feathered headdresses, it was wonderful to see. We walked again from morning to night, dancing and partying. The company we had signed up with provided moving bars, toilets and emergency services. They also provided lunch for us. If you ever go to Trinidad, I highly recommend trying the delicious bake n' shark which is fried fish in flatbread. Try it with any of the sauces provided. I had it with a red pepper sauce and it was spicy and delicious.

It was after 7:30 pm and the parade was passing close to our hotel. By now, we had been walking for almost 10 hours all over Port of Spain. Hubby and I threw in the towel and returned to our hotel. We heard later that the Carnival and afterparty continued for hours after we left. I don't know how they did it.

Our feet hurt badly but the overarching emotion was elation at having been a part of something incredible. After long hot showers, we massaged each other's feet, but it was a few days before I stopped walking gingerly. The next day was spent recovering from the parades and parties.

It was a great way to end my trip around the world. It was the realization of yet another dream. It turns out all you need to achieve your dreams is go after them. Given half a chance, I would join thousands of people and return to Trinidad for Carnival.

Carnival

To prepare for Carnival in Trinidad

- It goes without saying, book early. Start minimum a year in advance. Hotels and costumes sell out quickly.

- Book a place to stay along the parade route. The feeling when you are exhausted and you look up and see your hotel just beyond the parade is priceless. Some hotels have shuttles that take you to the parade route also.

- Get a concierge service. They will buy and pick up your costume, book parties for you, and take you to them.

- Bring comfortable walking shoes and insoles. Bring heating pads for your feet for after the parade. Your feet will thank you.

- For girls: bring tights, make up, body jewels, glitter, fake lashes, etc. and the associated glues needed. You don't want to feel left out. Don't wear toeless tights. The holes pull against your toes during the parade and make your feet hurt even worse.

- You don't need to walk all day on Monday. That's the day when most people don't wear their costumes. Tuesday is the proper parade day. If you walk from 10 am to 7 pm on Monday, you may be too tired for Tuesday.

- Don't bother learning the carnival songs in advance. They are played at all parties and throughout the parades. I promise, you will know the words soon enough. Primarily, soca music is played. Learn how to dance to it.

- For girls: be sure to bring padding to fill up your bra top in case it is too big. I had to use tissues and they worked ok until I started sweating.

- Ensure you have enough space in your suitcase to pack your costume for your return home.

THE END

It took a while to get used to being back home. I was glad to be done with travels. I think any longer than three months and I would have started taking travel for granted. It would have lost its special feeling. I did miss meeting new people every day, and experiencing new things regularly. I have to keep reminding myself that there are plenty of people I don't know where I live.

As one of my cab drivers in London said, every place has something special about it. Antarctica and Morocco were my favorite stops. Both have incredible natural beauty: icebergs and penguins, dunes and camels. Morocco wins out as my favorite place on earth because of how incredibly kind and generous the people are. The country's history and culture make it even more special. And of course, the Sahara is where I made peace with myself.

Hong Kong had the most interesting food. Mozambique had the best seafood. Thailand had the best food overall, hands down.

FROM ANTARCTICA TO ZIMBABWE

Madrid, Spain was peaceful and quiet, and a great place to recover from my adventures in Antarctica.

The UAE was the most opulent place I have ever visited. Bora Bora had the bluest water I've ever seen.

Tahiti is where I experienced crossing the International Date Line for the first time.

In Australia, I played music with Aborigines.

In Singapore, I experienced the hope of an entire nation.

In England, Zimbabwe and Italy, I experienced history through monuments left by our ancestors.

In Argentina, where my trip started, I marveled at the Andes looking down on us from their lofty perch.

In the Netherlands, I glimpsed Amsterdam from canals surrounding the city.

In Cameroon, I spent quality time with my family.

In Rwanda, I communed with gorillas.

In Namibia, I sand-boarded in the Namib Desert.

In Swaziland, I experienced the most breathtaking view over breakfast.

In Malaysia, I experienced generosity showed by an old friend through his family.

In South Africa, I was nearly overwhelmed by mountain and ocean views in Cape Town.

In Lesotho, I experienced some parts of the life of a Sotho woman, including delicious fresh baked bread.

In Trinidad, I partied like a rock star in frills and feathers.

In the US, I visited Hollywood where movie stars are made.

But it was my time in Zambia that was the most influential on the rest of my life. Seeing how my friend Susie lived really inspired me to go into business for myself. I loved the flexibility that her life choices afforded her. I could see myself living the same way, working when I wanted to, then traveling when I am tired of work, without needing permission from anyone. In fact, I vowed never to do anything I don't want to do. In the months since, I have turned down opportunities that didn't feel "right," as I didn't want to compromise my vision for myself.

I had a lot of "F*@# this sh*t" moments because I knew what I wanted and I learned to move away from anything that didn't get me closer to those things. My experience with Kibs was heartbreaking because I lost a friend. But maybe it was time for that friendship to be over. The Kibs I traveled with is not someone I would choose to be friends with today.

Everything I wanted to do, I made happen. This was a huge lesson for me, a reminder that if I want something, I should just go for it.

I successfully traveled to all seven continents, in three and a half months, and all by myself. My trip around the world wasn't to prove anything to myself. I wasn't trying to find myself or anything like that. It was traveling for the sake of traveling. Having said that, I did find myself out there in the world. I learned a lot of things, both good and bad, about myself.

I learned that stone is forever as evidenced by Great Zimbabwe and Stonehenge. I learned that a lot of exertion is required to experience things and many times I asked myself if what I was doing was worth the effort it was taking. The answer was yes, every time. I also learned that dirt washes off. A lot of my experiences required me to get down and dirty, for instance the gorilla trek. I made many friends, and I lost at least one.

I was careful at times and reckless at other times. I was charged by a silverback gorilla, I was on a ship that hit an iceberg, I got stranded in the Sahara Desert, and I almost drowned in the Pacific Ocean. Yet, I did amazing things too. I visited Antarctica, I meditated in the Sahara Desert, I sand-boarded in the Namib Desert, and I participated in Carnival, costume and all.

I was lucky enough and I planned carefully enough that I never encountered bedbugs, I never got robbed, I never fell sick, and my luggage was never lost. I was treated with kindness everywhere I went in the world. That taught me that people are fundamentally good, no matter what the media would like us to believe.

Traveling for so long taught me to pick my battles or else I would have missed irreplaceable moments. It also taught me that the journey is just as important as the destination.

I learned that we need a break every now and again to replenish our spirits and find ourselves.

Most importantly, traveling showed me that

> If I want something, the worst thing I can do is not try for it.

I am applying this to all aspects of my life, starting with writing this book. I met a lot of interesting people who showed me that there is more than one way to live life. So rather than fall into old patterns, I am designing my life the way I actually want to live it. I don't expect to always succeed, but I have to at least try. And if I accidentally end up in the wrong place, or doing the wrong thing, I quickly make a decision and say,

"F*@# this sh*t."

www.ingramcontent.com/pod-product-compliance
Lightning Source LLC
Chambersburg PA
CBHW071603080526
44588CB00010B/1004